Jesus Is Coming Soon?

by
Jim Reeves

First Edition Design Publishing
Sarasota, Florida USA

Jesus Is Coming Soon?
Copyright ©2016 Jim Reeves

ISBN 978-1506-912-30-1 PRINT
ISBN 978-1506-902-52-4 EBOOK

LCCN 2016945322

June 2016

Published and Distributed by
First Edition Design Publishing, Inc.
P.O. Box 20217, Sarasota, FL 34276-3217
www.firsteditiondesignpublishing.com

ALL RIGHTS RESERVED. No part of this book publication may be reproduced, stored in a retrieval system, or transmitted in any form or by any means — electronic, mechanical, photo-copy, recording, or any other — except brief quotation in reviews, without the prior permission of the author or publisher.

All Scripture quotations, unless otherwise indicated, are taken from the *Holy Bible,*

New International Version®. *NIV*™. Copyright © 1973, 1978, 1984 by International

Bible Society. Used by permission of Zondervan. All rights reserved.

From the cowardice that shrinks from new truth,

From the laziness that is content with half-truth,

From the arrogance that thinks it knows all truth,

O God of Truth, deliver us!

~ Ancient Prayer

TABLE OF CONTENTS

Introduction 1

Chapter 1 Understanding God's Time 7
Chapter 2 The Time Of The End 23
Chapter 3 The Last Days 33
Chapter 4 The End Of The World 51
Chapter 5 The Atonement Sacrifice 69
Chapter 6 The Kingdom Of Heaven 85
Chapter 7 What Did Jesus Really Say? 101
Conclusion So What's Next? 125

About The Author 127

Introduction

Jesus is coming soon? Of all the adjectives that might be used to describe one's expectations about the second coming of Jesus, if he has not come in over 2000 years, *soon* is certainly not one of them. Yet, it was Jesus who said he was coming *soon*. If he did not return as promised, he was not the Son of God and Christianity is a false religion. It may surprise you to know that Jesus explained in easily understandable terms exactly when and why he was coming back...soon.

The Bible is the most incredible book ever written. It has been translated into virtually every language in the world and, although it is impossible to know the exact number of copies in print, recent estimates put the total between five and six billion copies! Without question it is the most renowned and influential literature ever produced. It has been the guiding force for individuals and nations, has been the basis for constitutions and governments, and has greatly influenced all civilization.

It is also the most controversial book ever written. Some, including this author, view the Bible as the divinely inspired, infallible word of the Almighty God. Some see it as a book of interesting stories and fables; others consider it just one of many good books containing worthwhile moral principles and religious teachings, while many believe it to be the greatest hoax ever perpetrated on mankind.

One's view of the Bible depends entirely on how well he or she understands its contents. It is not just a collection of unrelated writings from many authors about various subjects and periods of history. It is one consistent story written by 40 different people over a period of almost 1500 years. Many of the Old Testament

Introduction

books contain prophecies of things that would happen hundreds of years in the future, yet every one of them happened exactly when and how they were predicted. Much of the New Testament is an explanation of how all the Old Testament prophecies were fulfilled, primarily in the person and work of Jesus Christ. Every book of the Bible is a part of one story...how God would redeem mankind from the consequences of sin. It is the most exciting and incredible story ever told.

That a book could be written over such a long period of time by so many different people about one story and contain no inconsistencies or contradictions is part of the overwhelming evidence that the Bible is the inspired word of the living God. People who choose not to believe in God are quick to point out all the differences and contradictions in doctrines taught by those who claim to be Christians and followers of the Scriptures. Their claims are based, not on what the Bible actually says, but on what different religious teachers say it says.

No religious subject has cast more doubt on the authenticity of the Holy Scriptures, nor caused more harm to the church of Jesus Christ, than modern interpretations of what is referred to by many as the "second coming of Christ." That Jesus said he was going to come again is a fact that cannot be disputed. **When** and **why** he said he would return are the points of all the misunderstanding and confusion. Our failure to properly study and understand the Scriptures that refer to the "last days," the "coming of the Lord" and many other such terms have led to a plethora of false ideas and teachings, even among Christian churches.

Atheists are quick to point out the inconsistency in our theology and denounce Christianity as a false religion and Jesus as a fake. Even many Christian writers publically say the apostles misunderstood Jesus and were mistaken in their belief about the timing of his coming. In his essay, *The World's Last Night*, the renowned Christian writer C. S. Lewis wrote the following in 1960:

> "Say what you like, the apocalyptic beliefs of the first Christians have been proven to be false. It is clear from the New Testament that they all expected the Second Coming in their own lifetime. And, worse still, they had a reason, and one you will find very embarrassing. Their Master had told them so. He shared, and indeed created, their delusion. He said in so many words, *'this generation shall not pass till all these things be done.'* And He was wrong. He clearly knew no more about the end of the world than anyone else. It is certainly the most embarrassing verse in the Bible."

Lewis is correct in his assessment of what Jesus said and what his disciples believed. Eschatology (a study of the "end times") is no insignificant subject in the Scriptures. The imminent return of Jesus is a consistent, recurring theme throughout the entire New Testament. Many sincere people, in an effort to explain why they believe he did not returned as expected, have come up with a variety of explanations. Predictions of Jesus' return have become commonplace and they have all proven to be false. The prevalent "left behind" philosophy proclaimed by most Christian churches today is simply not supported by Scripture and undermines the credibility of God and his word.

Perhaps we should look more closely at what the Scriptures actually say. Jesus and the apostles not only explained when the Lord would return, but they also explained why his return was necessary. His "second coming" was an integral part of the atonement sacrifice and fits perfectly within the overall story of redemption. If we understand *why* Jesus said he would return then we will understand *when* he said he was coming.

Introduction

Christians have a mission with a message. Like Moses speaking to the Israelites before they entered the Promised Land, we set before the world a life and death choice. It is a positive message of hope because one can choose life. But it is also a choice based on reason and understanding. This challenge was the conclusion of Moses' message in Deuteronomy 30. At the beginning of the previous chapter we read, *"Your eyes have seen all that the Lord did in Egypt to Pharaoh, to all his officials and to all his land. With your own eyes you saw those great trials, those miraculous signs and great wonders. But to this day the Lord has not given you a mind that understands or eyes that see or ears that hear. During the forty years that I led you through the desert, your clothes did not wear out, nor did the sandals on your feet. You ate no bread and drank no wine or other fermented drink. I did this so that you might know that I am the Lord your God"* (Deuteronomy 29:1-6). He goes on to tell them of one thing after another they had witnessed proving the goodness and faithfulness of God. Then, based on all the evidence, he tells them to choose between this faithful God who had led them from Egypt and through the wilderness for the past forty years, or the gods in the land they would soon enter.

What if Moses had promised them God was going to part the Red Sea, but it had never happened? What if Moses had promised them God would send meat in the wilderness, but it had never come? What if, after spending 40 years in the wilderness, they were not able to cross the Jordan River and move into the land God had promised them? Suppose Moses kept trying to explain to them God was going to do what he promised…SOME DAY? Now suppose those promises had not come to pass after thousands of years? How much credibility would Moses or his God have? Would there be any reason to "choose life" when other things that had been promised never came to pass?

That is precisely what is happening in the world today with the message of the gospel of Christ. Rather than hearing the simple truth of the Gospel and a reasonable, understandable and consistent explanation of Scripture, the world has witnessed decades of confused doctrine and failed prophecies. Moses based his plea for people to choose life on the faithfulness of God to keep his word. If people today, listening to television evangelists and a growing list of other preachers and teachers who make endless promises and prophecies that never come true, use the same criteria to judge the message of the modern church, how can anyone reasonably expect them to choose life? Only by getting back to the Bible and presenting God's complete, understandable message can there be any hope of fulfilling our mission.

2 Corinthians 5:17-21, *"Therefore, if anyone is in Christ, he is a new creation; the old has gone, the new has come! All this is from God, who reconciled us to himself through Christ and gave us the ministry of reconciliation: that God was reconciling the world to himself in Christ, not counting men's sins against them. And he has committed to us the message of reconciliation. We are therefore Christ's ambassadors, as though God were making his appeal through us. We implore you on Christ's behalf: Be reconciled to God. God made him who had no sin to be sin for us, so that in him we might become the righteousness of God."* We will not reconcile the world to God until we reconcile our own beliefs and doctrine with his word.

The confusion does not lie with the Scriptures. The Lord's coming, about which Jesus and the New Testament writers taught, is not difficult to understand if we will simply believe what the Bible says. The apostles were not mistaken about the timing of the Lord's coming. Jesus did know what he was talking about. The embarrassment is for C. S. Lewis, the scoffers and false teachers of the first century, and all the others who proclaim something other than what the Bible so clearly teaches.

The purpose of this book is to serve as an introduction to what the Bible actually says about the "second coming" of Christ and other events of the "end times" and to encourage more study of the Scriptures. As the apostle Paul wrote to the Ephesian Christians, it is my prayer *"that the God of our Lord Jesus Christ, the glorious Father, may give you the Spirit of wisdom and revelation, so that you may know him better. I pray that the eyes of your heart may be enlightened in order that you may know the hope to which he has called you, the riches of his glorious inheritance in his holy people, and his incomparably great power for us who believe."*

CHAPTER 1

Understanding God's Time

Does what one believes concerning the Biblical "end times" really matter? Many will say it does not and are not even interested in hearing or studying about it. But it does matter. Why? First and foremost, it matters because Jesus taught about it in great detail. He linked his "second coming" to the end of the old law and the establishment of the new covenant of grace, to the fulfillment of all Old Testament prophesies, to his atonement for sin as our High Priest, to the work of the Holy Spirit in revealing God's will to the writers of the New Testament, and to the establishment of the kingdom of heaven. It mattered a great deal to Jesus.

It matters because it is a major theme throughout the writings of the apostles and other New Testament authors. The "soon coming of the Lord" was taught to all first century Christians to warn them of the trials they were facing in their very near future and to assure them that God was always faithful to his promises and would see them through this time. If it was important enough to be a topic in virtually every New Testament book, it should matter to us.

It matters because it has a significant impact on how the world views God, the Bible, and the church. Christians should present a positive, hopeful message to the world. The word "gospel" means good news. That the world is bad and only going to get worse and we are facing "terrible times in the last days" and are soon going to see a time of horrible "tribulation" until God finally destroys the universe and everything in it does not sound like good news! Forgiveness and redemption is the message of the Bible from beginning to end…not gloom, doom and destruction.

It also matters because people in the world can easily see that the multitude of prophesies about the "second coming" and the "end of the world" over the past two centuries have all proven to be false. How many times can Christians shout "the sky is falling" before everyone begins to see this "chicken little" message for exactly what it is? Modern interpretations of Jesus' statements that he is "coming soon," whether in the form of false prophesies about the end of the world or attempts to explain why Jesus did not mean what he said, serve only to undermine the faithfulness of God and his word.

Instead of some cataclysmic destruction of the universe, consider for a moment, if the "end times" passages in Scripture refer to the end of a physical kingdom so that the spiritual kingdom of heaven could come to fruition; the end of the Law of Moses so the grace of God through Jesus Christ could be the basis of his judgement; the end of animal sacrifices because our atonement was finally complete with the blood of a sinless Savior…would that not truly be good news? God's concern and plan for the world is, always has been, and always will be, its salvation, not its destruction. Understanding what Jesus and his apostles taught concerning the "end times" does really matter.

In order to comprehend what the Scriptures teach about the "end times" one must understand that from the time Adam and Eve first sinned in the Garden of Eden, God set in motion his plan for atonement so mankind could be forgiven and redeemed. This plan unfolded over several centuries and is the underlying subject of every book of the Bible. Beginning in Genesis 3:16 God promised Satan, *"I will put enmity between you and the woman, and between your offspring and hers; he will crush your head, and you will strike his heel."* The "he" in this passage refers to Jesus who would eventually be born of woman and make atonement for all sin, dealing the crushing fatal blow to Satan.

Jesus is Coming Soon?

The problem facing mankind has always been sin. The result of sin is death...spiritual death, separation from the eternal God who is life. Jesus said, *"I am the way, the truth, and the life"* (John 14:6). The apostle Paul repeatedly wrote that we are dead in sin, but made alive in Christ. Sin has always separated man from God. Isaiah said in chapter 59:1-2, *"Surely the arm of the Lord is not too short to save, nor his ear too dull to hear. But your iniquities have separated you from your God; your sins have hidden his face from you, so that he will not hear."* The story of the Bible is what God did about the problem of sin. Adam and Eve chose to sin. Even though they knew the consequences beforehand, they still made that choice. Living in paradise was not sufficient motivation for them to always obey God. They sinned...they died. But God did promise to do something about the sin problem in the future.

The story of the flood in Genesis 6-9 is not just some unrelated story about a man who built a boat and saved a lot of animals. It is a graphic illustration not only of the consequences of sin but also the futility of trying to physically remove it from the earth...even by very drastic means. Even though people were created in the image of God, they were given the freedom in their own lives to make their own choices. All of us sometimes make the wrong choices. Following the flood men and women still were free to make their own choices...and they often chose sin over obedience to God. In Genesis 8:21 God again made a promise; *"Never again will I curse the ground because of humans, even though every inclination of the human heart is evil from childhood. And never again will I destroy all living creatures, as I have done."* God promised he would never again destroy all living creatures because of sin. The answer to the sin problem was not annihilation. There had to be a better solution.

In Genesis 12 God called a man named Abram to separate himself and his immediate family from the other nations and he would become the father of a great nation. Later the Lord changed his name to Abraham in Genesis 18:18 God said, *"Abraham will surely become a great and powerful nation, and all nations on earth will be blessed through him."* Abraham did not live to see the ultimate fulfillment of this promise during his lifetime and, for many more generations, there was still no solution to the sin problem. However, we know through him, Isaac, Jacob and their many other descendants Jesus was eventually born into the world. God was true to his promise and through Abraham's seed all nations were and are indeed blessed.

As the story of Abraham and his descendants unfolds in the Bible, we find they eventually had to go live in Egypt to survive a terrible famine. After a number of good years, a new pharaoh began to rule and the living conditions of the Israelites, as they had begun to be known, quickly degenerated into slavery. Like everything else in God's plan, their bondage in Egypt and miraculous delivery by God's power was symbolic of an even greater event that would occur many generations in the future. All of mankind was in bondage to sin and only a great deliverer could bring freedom.

Once the Israelites crossed the sea into the wilderness, safe from the Egyptian army, God called Moses up Mount Sinai and gave him the Ten Commandments along with all the other regulations of what became known as the Law of Moses. Because people were unable to keep the Law perfectly, it still did not solve the problem of sin. Animal sacrifices offered annually by the High Priest were insufficient to make atonement for sin, but they were a symbol of the One who was coming who could do that once and for all. The Old Testament books of Law, along with the Psalms and Prophets, all pointed to a coming Messiah who would finally make atonement for sin by sacrificing his own blood.

And, when God's time was finally right…JESUS CAME.

He came exactly when, where, and how God had said he would. Thousands of years of history and prophecies pointed to the exact time and place where Jesus would be born...and die. When he was only 33 years old, after three short years of personal ministry and teaching, Jesus was betrayed, arrested, falsely accused, beaten, forsaken, crucified and died. Three days later, just as he had promised, he arose from the grave. Everything about Jesus' birth, life, death, and resurrection happened precisely as, and when, the Holy Scriptures said it would. But God's eternal plan was not yet complete. And just prior to his crucifixion Jesus made some astonishing statements concerning another future event.

He was coming again!

Like everything else in God's plan, this was not anything new for those listening who understood the Scriptures. The same prophecies that had so accurately predicted his birth and death also predicted this second coming with the same pinpoint accuracy. If we invest the time and effort to understand the Old Testament prophecies we will also have no trouble understanding what Jesus and his apostles taught about the Lord's future coming.

Let's start with the obvious. Did Jesus say when he was coming back? You may be surprised to know the answer is absolutely "yes". He not only told them when he was coming back but also told them exactly how to know for sure when it happened. There would be signs that nobody could miss.

In Matthew 24:1-3, *Jesus left the temple and was walking away when his disciples came up to him to call his attention to its buildings. "Do you see all these things?" he asked. "Truly I tell you, not one stone here will be left on another; every one will be thrown down." As Jesus was sitting on the Mount of Olives, the disciples came to him privately. "Tell us," they said, "when will this happen, and what will be the sign of your coming and of the end of the age?"*

Consider carefully the context of Matthew 24. Jesus was answering a question his disciples had asked. The specific discussion they had just had was about the temple and surrounding buildings. These buildings were the most magnificent structures in the world. When the original temple was built by King Solomon, people came from all over the world to marvel at its splendor. To the apostles and all Jews of that time the temple was also the most holy place on earth. After all, it contained the one place, called the Holy of Holies, where the High Priest went once each year to offer the blood of the atonement sacrifices. This was as close as any human could ever get to actually being in the presence of God.

One can only imagine their astonishment when Jesus said that it was going to be totally destroyed. They wanted to know when this was going to happen and what sign to watch for so they would know it was about to take place. The disciples had read and been taught the Old Testament Scriptures from birth. They knew there was a coming Messiah and they believed Jesus was that promised redeemer. They also knew from Scripture that when the Messiah came, he would establish a new kingdom, with a new temple, not built by human hands, but by the Lord himself. They also knew from Scripture that would all happen at the end of the age.

We will look more in depth at all these concepts later in our study, but knowing what they believed from their knowledge of the Scriptures, we can understand their question. "When was the temple going to be destroyed, and what will be the sign of your coming and the end of the age?" The disciples were not asking three unrelated questions about three different events in history thousands of years apart. They were asking about only one future event; the destruction of the temple in Jerusalem, which they knew would have age-changing consequences. It is important to note they asked when would be the end of the *age*...not the end of the world.

And Jesus answered their question. He continued his conversation with them telling them of all the signs that would indicate the time for this historic event was drawing closer, right up to the time it would happen. Beginning in verse 30 he said, *"Then will appear the sign of the Son of Man in heaven. And then all the peoples of the earth will mourn when they see the Son of Man coming on the clouds of heaven, with power and great glory. And he will send his angels with a loud trumpet call, and they will gather his elect from the four winds, from one end of the heavens to the other. Now learn this lesson from the fig tree: As soon as its twigs get tender and its leaves come out, you know that summer is near. Even so, when you see all these things, you know that it is near, right at the door. Truly I tell you,* **this generation will certainly not pass away until all these things have happened.***"* Jesus said he would return in that generation.

It also helps to look at the other accounts of this same conversation. Three of the gospel writers included this discussion between Jesus and his disciples. Mark phrased the disciples' question this way in chapter 13 verse 4; *"Tell us, when will these things happen? And what will be the sign that they are all about to be fulfilled?"* And Luke 21:7 says, *"Teacher," they asked, "when will these things happen? And what will be the sign that they are about to take place?"* It is obvious from these two other accounts of that same conversation the disciples were asking about only one future event.

Matthew and Mark were educated Jews who had a very thorough knowledge of the Old Testament Scriptures. Their gospels were written to Jews, so they naturally said things in a way that another Jew, with similar knowledge of the Scriptures, would understand. Luke was most likely a gentile, writing to another gentile. His gospel does not assume the reader understands the Old Testament, so he phrases some things differently. For instance, Matthew 24:15-16 says, *"So when you see standing in the holy place 'the abomination that causes desolation,' spoken of through the prophet Daniel—let the reader understand— then let those who are in Judea flee to the mountains."* Luke 21:20-22 uses different words to say exactly the same thing, *"When you see Jerusalem being surrounded by armies, you will know that its desolation is near. Then let those who are in Judea flee to the mountains, let those in the city get out, and let those in the country not enter the city. For this is the time of punishment in fulfillment of all that has been written."*

All three gospel writers record Jesus' direct answer to the question the disciples asked. *"This generation will certainly not pass away until all these things have happened."* Jesus had told them this before. In Matthew 16:28 Jesus said, *"I tell you the truth, some who are standing here will not taste death before they see the Son of Man coming in his kingdom."*

Jesus said he would return, and the temple would be destroyed, during the generation in which they were currently living at that time…not some thousands (or millions) of years in the future. He said some living at that time would still be alive to see his return!

But when did the apostles and other New Testament writers say Jesus would return? The Apostle Paul wrote in great detail about the Lord's coming and he understood and taught very clearly that it was going to happen soon, in the very near future (his near future, not ours). In 1 Corinthians 7 he said, *"What I mean, brothers and sisters, is that* **the time is short***…For this world in its present form is passing away."* All the other writers of the New Testament say exactly the same thing.

> James 5:7-9, *"Be patient, then, brothers, until the Lord's coming. See how the farmer waits for the land to yield its valuable crop and how patient he is for the autumn and spring rains. You too, be patient and stand firm,* **because the Lord's coming is near.** *Don't grumble against each other, brothers, or you will be judged.* **The Judge is standing at the door!"**

1 Peter 4:7, *"**The end of all things is near.** Therefore be clear minded and self-controlled so that you can pray."*

1 John 2:18, *"Dear children, **this is the last hour;** and as you have heard that the antichrist is coming, even now many antichrists have come. **This is how we know it is the last hour.**"*

Hebrews 10:35-37, *"So do not throw away your confidence; it will be richly rewarded.*

*You need to persevere so that when you have done the will of God, you will receive what he has promised. For in **just a very little while** (literally soon, very soon), he who is coming will come and will not delay."*

Revelation 1:1-3, *"The revelation of Jesus Christ, which God gave him to show his servants **what must soon take place.** He made it known by sending his angel to his servant John, who testifies to everything he saw-that is, the word of God and the testimony of Jesus Christ. Blessed is the one who reads the words of this prophecy, and blessed are those who hear it and take to heart what is written in it, **because the time is near.**"*

Revelation 3:10, *"Since you have kept my command to endure patiently, I will also keep you from the **hour of trial that is going to come upon the whole world** to test those who live on the earth."* If the trial that was coming on the world was not to come for at least two centuries, this promise to keep these first century Christians safe from it would have been meaningless.

Revelation 22:6-10, *"The angel said to me, 'These words are trustworthy and true. The Lord, the God of the spirits of the prophets, sent his angel to show his servants the **things that must soon take place. Behold, I am coming soon!** Blessed is he who keeps the words of the prophecy in this book.' I, John, am the one who heard and saw these things. And when I had heard and seen them, I fell down to worship at the feet of the angel who had been showing them to me. But he said to me, 'Do not do it! I am a fellow servant with you and with your brothers the prophets and of all who keep the words of this book. Worship God!' Then he told me, '**Do not seal up the words of the prophecy of this book, because the time is near.**'"*

Revelation 22:12, *"**Behold, I am coming soon!** My reward is with me, and I will give to everyone according to what he has done."*

Revelation 22:20, *"He who testifies to these things says, '**Yes, I am coming soon.**' Amen. **Come, Lord Jesus.**"*

When does every instance in the New Testament where it is mentioned say Jesus was coming back? SOON! What part of "soon" do we not understand? Over two thousand years is not soon.

Jesus is Coming Soon?

"Jesus is coming soon" was true in the first century. It is not true today!

C. S. Lewis was absolutely correct in his assessment that "It is clear from the New Testament that they all expected the Second Coming in their own lifetime...Their Master had told them so." So why have religious teachers spent so much time and effort trying to interpret the Scriptures to support a yet future coming of Jesus that is neither taught, nor even mentioned in the Bible?

We can only speculate what other people think or what their motives are, however one can assume that most religious leaders today, just like their counterparts in the first century, tend to interpret the Scriptures to support their preconceived ideas of what they believe the coming of the Messiah should be like. The Jews of Jesus' day missed their Messiah because they were expecting a physical kingdom, not the spiritual one that had been prophesied and which Jesus came to establish. Little has changed in two thousand years.

Why can we not just simply believe what the Bible actually says? The Scriptures contain a lot of statements, promises and prophesies that include time references. In every case, without exception, everything happened exactly how and *when* God said it would. In Numbers 14 he promised the children of Israel would wander in the wilderness for forty years, one year for each day the spies spent checking out the land beyond the Jordan River. They spent exactly forty years in the wilderness.

In Jeremiah 25 we read where God was going to have the people of Judah taken captive by Babylon because of their sin and rebellion. The Lord told them they would serve the king of Babylon for seventy years. Then in Jeremiah 29:10 God promised, *"This is what the Lord says: 'When seventy years are completed for Babylon, I will come to you and fulfill my good promise to bring you back to this place. For I know the plans I have for you.' "* Then in

Daniel 9:1-3 we read, *"In the first year of Darius son of Xerxes (a Mede by descent), who was made ruler over the Babylonian kingdom— in the first year of his reign, I, Daniel, understood from the Scriptures, according to the word of the Lord given to Jeremiah the prophet, that the desolation of Jerusalem would last seventy years. So I turned to the Lord God and pleaded with him in prayer and petition, in fasting, and in sackcloth and ashes."* Daniel was living in Babylon, but he knew from Scripture that the Israelites would be returning to Judah as soon as the seventy years were complete. And they did.

When God says forty years, he means exactly forty years…when he says seventy years, he means exactly seventy years. Many other examples could be given, but the simple truth is God communicates with people in time we can understand. If he says something will happen in a certain generation, he means exactly that. If he says it will be soon…it makes no sense to say it may be thousands of years in the future.

Yet, when it comes to the "second coming," in an effort to explain the statements of Jesus and the very obvious expectations of the apostles, many religious teachers claim that one cannot take God literally when it comes to time, since he does not live in our time. The most quoted passage to support this view is 2 Peter 3:8-9. Here the Apostle Peter says, *"But do not forget this one thing, dear friends: With the Lord a day is like a thousand years, and a thousand years are like a day. The Lord is not slow in keeping his promise, as some understand slowness. Instead he is patient with you, not wanting anyone to perish, but everyone to come to repentance."*

The concept Peter is explaining to his readers is that God remembers a thousand years as easily as we remember one day. This same point is made repeatedly throughout Scripture. Psalm 105:7-10 says, *"He is the Lord our God; his judgments are in all the earth. He remembers his covenant forever, the word he commanded, for a thousand generations, the covenant he made with Abraham, the oath he swore to Isaac."* The point the psalmist is making is not that time means nothing to God. He is saying God never forgets what he has promised. Time statements are just as important to God as anything else he says. And he always keeps his word.

Psalm 90:4, *"For a thousand years in your sight are like a day that has just gone by, or like a watch in the night."* The Apostle Peter, quoting from this Psalm, is not saying that when God says something will happen in "this generation" he may mean a thousand generations. The point the Psalmist and Peter made was that God will always be faithful to his promises.

In the context of 2 Peter there were people trying to cause doubt and confusion among the Christians by claiming that Jesus had not kept his promise to come when he had promised. At the time of Peter's writing it had been approximately 30 years since Jesus had told them *"this generation will not pass away until all these things* (including his coming in the clouds) *have happened."* In verses 3-4 Peter says, *"Above all, you must understand that in the last days scoffers will come, scoffing and following their own evil desires. They will say, Where is this 'coming' he promised? Ever since our ancestors died, everything goes on as it has since the beginning of creation."* These scoffers were claiming, as C.S. Lewis did, that Jesus did not know what he was talking about when he made the promise to come during that generation.

Peter's answer was to remind them of the flood of Noah's day. Imagine the scoffers of that time asking Noah, "Where is this rain your God promised?" But as Peter said, God kept his promise and the world was destroyed by water. Peter's point was if Jesus promised to return during that generation…he would. And he did!

When Jesus was explaining to his apostles what would happen to the temple and the signs that would indicate the time was approaching (Matt. 24:34, Mark 13:30, Luke 21:32), he spoke about all the following things:

1. Nation against nation wars
2. Famines and earthquakes
3. Apostles persecuted and put to death
4. People will betray each other
5. Many false prophets will appear to deceive people
6. Increase in wickedness
7. Gospel will be preached to the whole world
8. "Abomination that causes desolation" spoken by Daniel
9. Great distress unequaled before or after
10. False Christs will appear, perform miracles to deceive the elect
11. Coming of the Son of Man
12. Sun darkened, moon not give light, stars fall, heavenly bodies shaken
13. Son of Man will appear in sky
14. Son of Man coming on clouds of sky with power and great glory
15. Angels sent with loud trumpet call to gather elect

He follows this descriptive list *with "when you see **all these things**, you know that it is near, right at the door. I tell you the truth, this generation will certainly not pass away until **all these things** have happened."*

Many have tried to rationalize this statement of Jesus to mean something entirely different by "stretching" the meaning of "this generation" to some undetermined amount of time that could be centuries long. One cannot arbitrarily change the meaning of Jesus' words just because they do not believe what he said.

The Greek word for generation is "genea" from "ginomai" which means *begotten*. The literal meaning is:

"The whole multitude of men living at the same time." (Matt. 24:34, Mark 13:30, Luke 1:48, 21:32, Phil 2:15) Especially those of the Jewish race living at the same period. (Matt. 11:16) Transferred from people to the time in which they lived, the word came to mean an age, i.e. a period ordinarily occupied by each successive generation, say, of thirty or forty years. (Acts. 14:16, 15:21, Eph. 3:5, Col. 1:26, Gen. 15:16) The word "genea" is to be distinguished from "aion", as not denoting a period of unlimited duration" (Vines Expository Dictionary of New Testament Words).

All reputable translators agree with the meaning of the original text in this passage. Here are just a few different examples of how they translated Matthew 24:34:

"Verily I say unto you, this generation shall not pass till all these things be fulfilled." (KJV)

"I solemnly say to you, the present age will not pass away before all this takes place." (Williams)

"I tell you the truth, all these things will happen while the people of this time are still living." (New Century)

"Truly I say to you, this generation will not pass away till all things take place." (RSV)

"Truly, I tell you, this generation...that is, the whole multitude of people living at the same time, in a definite given period...will not pass away till all these things taken together take place." (Amplified)

"For sure, I tell you, the people of this day will not pass away before all these things have happened." (New Life Version)

Understanding God's Time

In Luke 9:26-27 Jesus said, *"If anyone is ashamed of me and my words, the Son of Man will be ashamed of him **when he comes in his glory and in the glory of the Father and of the holy angels.** I tell you the truth, **some who are standing here will not taste death before they see the kingdom of God.**"* In John 21:22, when Peter asked about John, Jesus answered, *"If I want him to remain alive until I return, what is that to you? You must follow me."* Because of this, the rumor spread among the brothers that this disciple would not die. But Jesus did not say that he would not die; he only said, *"If I want him to remain alive until I return, what is that to you?"* If it were not possible for John to remain alive until his return, Jesus would certainly have never said so. Actually John did remain alive until Jesus' return. God's plan was for John to write the Revelation, and to do so he had to be alive when *all these things* happened.

In spite of what people today may say, God has never used time statements to deceive people and cause them to believe something that is not true. Jesus did not make statements about which he knew nothing and his apostles were certainly not led by the Holy Spirit to believe and write about something that would not happen as promised. God can tell time…and his time is always right.

CHAPTER 2

The Time of the End

We hear a lot today about the "end of time" and the "end of the world." Religious leaders and pseudo scholars have been predicting what they believe to be Biblical "end time" events for generations. Every time something major happens in the world, especially in the Middle East, there will be another round of false predictions in an attempt to force Biblical prophesies into current history. The result is always the same. The world does not end and more people doubt the validity of the Bible. What should be questioned is the validity of these false prophets and their message of some imagined end of the world, which the Holy Scriptures do not support.

The book of Daniel is the most detailed description we have concerning the "end times." It gives a unique historical account of what will happen from the time of the Babylonian empire, during which Daniel lived, up to the end of the kingdom of Israel and the establishment of God's eternal kingdom, described by Jesus as the kingdom of heaven. Daniel explains exactly what was going to happen leading up to and during the "time of the end." Jesus quoted Daniel when he was explaining when he would return, so we know they both taught about the same period of time. It is important to remember that Daniel prophesied about the "time of the end" not the "end of time." There is a huge difference.

The Bible has a lot to say about the *time of the end,* but it never mentions the *end of time.*

The Time of the End

In the first part of chapter eight we read the account of a strange vision Daniel saw about a ram and a goat. In verse 16 Gabriel was told to explain the vision to Daniel. In verse 17 Daniel said, *"As he came near the place where I was standing, I was terrified and fell prostrate. 'Son of man,' he said to me, 'understand that the vision concerns the time of the end.'"* Then in verse 19, *"He said: 'I am going to tell you what will happen later in the time of wrath, because the vision concerns the appointed time of the end.'"* We see from this passage the "time of the end" was also called the "time of wrath." These phrases were used to refer to the same period of time in Israel's future.

Then in the next chapter Gabriel came to Daniel again while he was praying and said, *"Daniel, I have now come to give you insight and understanding. As soon as you began to pray, a word went out, which I have come to tell you, for you are highly esteemed. Therefore, consider the word and understand the vision: Seventy 'sevens' are decreed for your people and your holy city to finish transgression, to put an end to sin, to atone for wickedness, to bring in everlasting righteousness, to seal up vision and prophecy and to anoint the Most Holy Place."*

Gabriel makes clear to Daniel the vision concerns "your people" and "your holy city," clearly identifying the subject of the vision to be the future of the kingdom of Israel and the city of Jerusalem. Then in Daniel 9:26-27 Gabriel continues, *"After the sixty-two 'sevens,' the Anointed One will be cut off and will have nothing. The people of the ruler who will come will destroy the city and the sanctuary. The end will come like a flood: War will continue until the end, and desolations have been decreed. He will confirm a covenant with many for one 'seven.' In the middle of the 'seven' he will put an end to sacrifice and offering. And on a wing of the temple he will set up an abomination that causes desolation, until the end that is decreed is poured out on him."* The end that is being foretold is the end of the nation of Israel and the city of Jerusalem.

In chapter 10 Daniel has another vision of a man dressed in linen. Again the angel explains to him in verse 14, *"Now I have come to explain to you what will happen to your people in the future, for the vision concerns a time yet to come."* The events of Daniel's visions still concern what will happen to his people, the Jews, in the future.

As we follow the narrative through the book of Daniel, the subject never changes. Daniel is being shown what will happen to the kingdom of Israel and the city of Jerusalem in the future. These things will happen at the "appointed time" during the "time of the end" of the Jewish nation.

>Daniel 11:27, *"The two kings, with their hearts bent on evil, will sit at the same table and lie to each other, but to no avail, because the end will still come at the appointed time."*

>Daniel 11:35, *"Some of the wise will stumble, so that they may be refined, purified and made spotless until the time of the end, for it will still come at the appointed time."*

>Daniel 11:40, *"At the time of the end the king of the South will engage him in battle, and the king of the North will storm out against him with chariots and cavalry and a great fleet of ships. He will invade many countries and sweep through them like a flood."*

>Daniel 12:4, *"But you, Daniel, close up and seal the words of the scroll until the time of the end. Many will go here and there to increase knowledge."*

The Time of the End

> Daniel 12:9, *"He replied, Go your way, Daniel, because the words are closed up and sealed until the time of the end."*

> Daniel 12:13, *"As for you, go your way till the end. You will rest, and then at the end of the days you will rise to receive your allotted inheritance."*

Numerous other Scriptures in both the Old and New Testaments speak of this same time of the end. Habakkuk 2:3 says, *"For the revelation awaits an appointed time; it speaks of the end and will not prove false. Though it linger, wait for it; it will certainly come and will not delay."*

The final event of this "time of the end" would occur on a specific day in history known in Scripture as the "day of the Lord" when he would reveal his divine mystery of salvation at the consummation of the ages. Daniel was given two specific revelations that allow us to pinpoint with historical accuracy the exact timing of these events.

In Daniel 9 we read that the angel Gabriel was sent to give him insight and understanding into what he had seen. In verses 24-27 we read:

> *"Seventy 'sevens' are decreed for your people and your holy city to finish transgression, to put an end to sin, to atone for wickedness, to bring in everlasting righteousness, to seal up vision and prophecy and to anoint the most holy.*

> *Know and understand this: From the issuing of the decree to restore and rebuild Jerusalem until the Anointed One, the ruler, comes, there will be seven 'sevens,' and sixty-two 'sevens.' It will be rebuilt with streets and a trench, but in times of trouble. After the*

sixty-two 'sevens,' the Anointed One will be cut off and will have nothing. The people of the ruler who will come will destroy the city and the sanctuary. The end will come like a flood: War will continue until the end, and desolations have been decreed. He will confirm a covenant with many for one 'seven.' In the middle of the 'seven' he will put an end to sacrifice and offering. And on a wing of the temple he will set up an abomination that causes desolation, until the end that is decreed is poured out on him."

The Hebrew word for "sevens" (translated "weeks" in some versions) means a unit of seven of something; much like the English word "dozen" means twelve of something. In this case, the prophecy concerns seventy seven-year periods of time, divided into three groups. The angel says there will be seven "sevens," or a period of 49 years, followed by sixty-two "sevens," or 434 years, followed by one 'seven,' or 7 years.

The time begins with *"...the issuing of the decree to restore and rebuild Jerusalem"* by Artaxerxes in 457 B.C. (Ezra 7:11-26). We read in Nehemiah how the rebuilding began with the wall of Jerusalem being completed in 52 days. The work was done in times of trouble, just as the angel had said to Daniel, with the workers carrying supplies in one hand and a sword in the other. Over the next 49 years the people of Israel rebuilt the city and surrounding communities and were resettled there.

According to the angel there would be a second period of 434 years, during which nothing specific was foretold. It was simply the time between the resettlement of Israel in and around Jerusalem and the beginning of the final 'seven'. He describes things that will happen "after the sixty-two sevens." Some of these occur during this final seven year period, and others are "decreed" during this time frame. When all of these events will have occurred, including the destruction of the "...city (Jerusalem) and the sanctuary (temple)," then *"...the end will come like a flood."*

According to Daniel, the events of this time frame leading up to "the end" would accomplish all of the following:
1. Finish transgression
2. Put an end to sin
3. Atone for wickedness
4. Bring in everlasting righteousness
5. Seal up vision and prophecy
6. Anoint the Most Holy

As we will see, these were all accomplished by Jesus during the "time of the end."

The final 'seven' in Gabriel's revelation to Daniel is divided into two segments. *"He will confirm a covenant with many for one 'seven.' In the middle of the 'seven' he will put an end to sacrifice and offering."* This seven year period begins with the baptism of Jesus and ends with the dispersion of the Jewish Christians following the stoning of Stephen. In the middle of this period Jesus is crucified, putting an end to sacrifice and offering.

Jesus had emptied himself of his heavenly glory and authority and had become human (Philippians 2:6-8, Hebrews 2:17) and was publicly declared to be the Son of God and "anointed" with the Holy Spirit at his baptism. Following his temptation by the Devil for forty days, he went back to Nazareth where he had lived as a child, stood up in the synagogue and read from Isaiah 61:1-2, *"'The Spirit of the Lord is on me, because he has anointed me to preach good news to the poor. He has sent me to proclaim freedom for the prisoners and recovery of sight for the blind, to release the oppressed, to proclaim the year of the Lord's favor.' Then he rolled up the scroll, gave it back to the attendant and sat down. The eyes of everyone in the synagogue were fastened on him, and he began by saying to them, 'Today this Scripture is fulfilled in your hearing'"* (Luke 4:18-21).

Beginning with his anointing, Jesus spent the next 3 ½ years teaching and "confirming" a new covenant with the people. His earthly ministry was confined to the people of Israel. During this time he not only taught about the coming kingdom of heaven, the church which he would build, but also carefully and in great detail explained (decreed) future events that would happen in that generation leading up to "the time of the end."

In the middle of this seven year period he was crucified. Following his death and resurrection the disciples were told to wait in Jerusalem for the Holy Spirit. For the next 3 ½ years their ministry was confined to Jerusalem and Judea, to the people of Israel. It was not until the stoning of Stephen that the gospel was taken to the Gentile world. This was to fulfill what had been prophesied that the word of the Lord would go out from Jerusalem. Jesus told the apostles they would be witnesses, beginning in Jerusalem, then Judea, then to the rest of the world. The covenant was confirmed with the Jews for a period of seven years and the "time of the end" had been decreed, just as Gabriel had explained to Daniel.

In the last three chapters of Daniel he is shown revelations and given explanations about the final events leading up to the "time of the end." In Chapter 10 he is shown a vision of an astonishing man who said, *"I have come to explain to you what will happen to your people in the future, for the vision concerns a time yet to come."* Through chapter 11 he once again takes Daniel through the coming, earthly kingdoms that will rise and fall before the final one that will destroy Jerusalem and its temple.

Speaking of this fourth kingdom (Roman) Daniel 11:31-32 says, *"His armed forces will rise up to desecrate the temple fortress and will abolish the daily sacrifice. Then they will set up the abomination that causes desolation."* Verse 35 says, *"Some of the wise will stumble so that they may be refined, purified and made spotless until the time of the end, for it will still come at the appointed time."*

"At the time of the end the king of the South will engage him in battle and the king of the North will storm out against him with chariots and cavalry and a great fleet of ships. He will invade many countries and sweep through them like a flood. He will invade the Beautiful Land" (Daniel 11:40-41). A study of the history of the Roman Jewish Wars between A.D. 66 and A.D. 70 shows a precise fulfillment of Daniel's prophesies.

> *"At that time Michael, the great prince who protects your people, will arise. There will be a time of distress such as has not happened from the beginning of nations until then. But at that time your people—everyone whose name is found written in the book—will be delivered. Multitudes who sleep in the dust of the earth will awake: some to everlasting life, others to shame and everlasting contempt. Those who are wise will shine like the brightness of the heavens, and those who lead many to righteousness, like the stars forever and ever. But you, Daniel, close up and seal the words of the scroll until the time of the end"* (Daniel 12:1-4).

When is this "time of the end"? Daniel identifies it as the time when the nation that rises to power following the Babylonians, Medes and Persians, and the Greeks invades the Beautiful Land, the home of his people, and sets up "the abomination that causes desolation" in the temple. He further describes it as *"...a time of distress such as has not happened from the beginning of nations until then."* Jesus clearly identifies these very same things as he "decrees" the signs that will precede the destruction of Jerusalem in his generation. The invading nation was Rome; the time was A. D. 70.

As Daniel looked up, he saw two more men standing on opposite banks of the Tigris River. One of them asked, *"How long will it be before these astonishing things are fulfilled?"* In the same figurative language used earlier in Daniel 7:25-28 the man answered, *"It will be for a time, times and half a time. When the power of the holy people has been finally broken, all these things will be completed."* Translated into years that would be 3 ½ years or 1,290 days.

We now have another 3 ½ year period during which there would be terrible times like never before or after leading up to the "time of the end." Exactly when would these days begin and end? Daniel gives us the answer.

"From the time that the daily sacrifice is abolished and the abomination that causes desolation is set up, there will be 1,290 days. Blessed is the one who waits for and reaches the end of the 1,335 days" (Daniel 12:11-12). Jesus confirmed this prophecy to be one of the signs of the impending destruction of Jerusalem and its temple and that it would happen during that generation.

From a historical standpoint we have the writings of Josephus, who witnessed these actual events. While not inspired Scripture, they give us an accurate historical account of what happened. Just as we can compare historical records with Daniel's prophesies about the four kingdoms with uncanny accuracy, so we see the same accuracy between the Scripture and the historical record of the Roman conquest of Judea and Jerusalem.

Josephus recorded in July of A.D. 66, in their rebellion against Rome, Jewish Zealots stormed Jerusalem, burned the palace of Agrippa and Bernice, killed Ananias, the High Priest, and killed a garrison of Roman soldiers. They stopped the twice-daily sacrifices that were being offered in the temple. Josephus identified the cessation of the daily sacrifices as the true beginning of the Roman-Jewish War.

Three-and-one-half years later (1290 days), in A.D. 70 Josephus records a major abomination in the temple. While the Roman army was encamped outside the city, three rival Jewish groups got embroiled in a bloody fight inside the temple for leadership control of the rebellion. The temple was a battleground, and the carnage filled every corner of the sacred building. Worshippers coming to offer sacrifices were murdered. Blood literally flowed out of the temple. Nothing like this had ever occurred before.

Forty-five days later, 1,335 days after the cessation of the daily sacrifice, the Roman army advanced into Jerusalem and began the final siege. The "time of the end" had come. By September of A.D. 70 not one stone was left on another.

The kingdom of Israel was established by God for one specific purpose; to bring the Messiah into the world. The eternal spiritual kingdom, which Jesus came to establish, was the primary plan from the beginning. God had told Abraham, the father of the nation of Israel, he would make of his offspring a great nation. He did. Yet he knew there was a spiritual dimension to God's promise that involved something much greater than a physical kingdom. Hebrews 11:8-10, *"By faith Abraham, when called to go to a place he would later receive as his inheritance, obeyed and went, even though he did not know where he was going. By faith he made his home in the promised land like a stranger in a foreign country; he lived in tents, as did Isaac and Jacob, who were heirs with him of the same promise. For he was looking forward to the city with foundations, whose architect and builder is God."*

In the Bible there were prophesies of an "end" and a "time of the end." Both of these referred to the coming end of the physical nation of Israel and the destruction of Jerusalem and its temple. As for the end of time…there is nothing in the Scriptures about that.

CHAPTER 3

The Last Days

An oft repeated statement among Christians today is that we are living in the "last days." This should evoke one obvious question - the last days of what? The Scriptures have a lot to say about events that will happen during the "last days" including the coming of Jesus in the clouds. In order for something to have last days, it must have an end. If we look closely at Scripture and keep it in its context, we will be able to determine that which was coming to an end and, therefore, had "last days." We will also be able to understand whether or not we are currently living in those days.

There is a very interesting parallel between the establishment of the physical kingdom of Israel and the establishment of the spiritual kingdom, the church. The physical kingdom was a prototype of the spiritual one that would follow. Every aspect of that first kingdom has its counterpart in the second. If we fail to understand the first, we will not understand the second. This is the reason it is so important for Christians to study and understand the Old Testament. It was God's physical demonstration of everything he was going to do in the spiritual kingdom.

Though the promise was made to Abraham years before, that physical kingdom actually began with deliverance from the bondage of slavery in Egypt, a prototype of man's bondage to sin. The crossing of the Red Sea and the physical destruction of the Egyptians (their captors) is a prototype of our baptism, whereby we symbolically accept God's deliverance from sin, our old "man of sin" is buried in the water, and we come out on the other side free from bondage. The High Priest and his offering of blood for the sins of the people is a prototype of Jesus and his atonement for our sins as a result of his perfect sacrifice on the cross. The Old Testament is a wealth of information that helps us better understand the spiritual kingdom into which we are "born again."

From the time the Israelites crossed the Red Sea until they entered the "promised land" was a period of forty years. These "first days" of the kingdom of Israel were accompanied by signs, miracles, and the outpouring of the Holy Spirit. Moses and a few others were given "miraculous gifts" that included graphic demonstrations to confirm his will, which was revealed during this period. This physical kingdom had "first days" and it also had "last days." The "last days" of physical Israel were also the "first days" of the spiritual kingdom, the church. This was also a period of forty years.

These "last days" of the old and "first days" of the new were from the baptism of Jesus by John the Baptist, an example of how we would be delivered from bondage and enter the new kingdom, to the literal destruction of Israel and its temple in A.D. 70 (40 years). Jesus clearly said the revealing of the kingdom of heaven (church) and the ending of the former kingdom began with John. In Matthew 11:12 he said, *"From the days of John the Baptist until now, the kingdom of heaven has been forcefully advancing, and forceful men lay hold of it. For all the Prophets and the Law prophesied until John."* Just like the beginning of the physical kingdom, the spiritual kingdom began with signs, wonders, and miraculous gifts of the Holy Spirit. During that forty year period the New Testament was revealed and God confirmed it with these miracles. This was the fulfillment of Micah's prophecy in chapter 7:15, *"As in the days when you came out of Egypt, I will show them my wonders."* And in Hebrews 1:1 the Bible says, *"In the past God spoke to our ancestors through the prophets at many times and in various ways, but **in these last days** he has spoken to us by his Son..."*

Then in chapter 2:3-4 it says, *"This salvation, which was first announced by the Lord, was confirmed to us by those who heard him. God also testified to it by signs, wonders and various miracles, and by gifts of the Holy Spirit distributed according to his will."*

The physical kingdom of Israel had a beginning and an end, first days and last days. The spiritual kingdom of heaven is eternal; it can have no "last days" because it will never end. "The end," of which the Bible speaks, is the end of the physical kingdom of Israel, not the end of the physical universe (See chart).

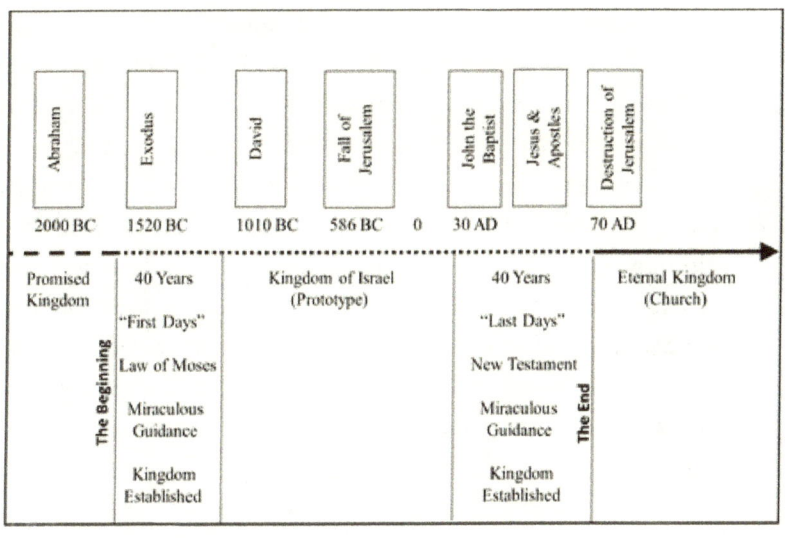

As a prototype of God's eternal kingdom, the nation of Israel had a beginning and an end. The "time of the end" about which Daniel prophesied was also known throughout Scripture as the "last days." The Bible is very clear about this time and what events would occur during these last days. The modern church is inundated with prophecies concerning these events and their "very soon" fulfillment. Books and movies fill the shelves at Christian bookstores telling in graphic detail what, in the minds of these modern prophets, is about to happen, and it is not a very comforting picture.

These doomsday prophets are certainly not without Scripture. There are some pretty scary things mentioned in the Bible concerning the "coming of the Lord," when there will be great calamity and destruction. In 2 Timothy 3:1 it says, *"But mark this: There will be terrible times in the last days."* In Matthew 24:21 Jesus said, *"There will be great distress, unequaled from the beginning of the world until now—and never to be equaled again."* Paul, in 1 Corinthians 7:31, *"For this world in its present form is passing away."* The Apostle Peter warned in 1 Peter 4:7, *"The end of all things is near."* And again in 2 Peter 3:10-11, *"But the day of the Lord will come like a thief. The heavens will disappear with a roar; the elements will be destroyed by fire, and the earth and everything in it will be laid bare. Since everything will be destroyed in this way, what kind of people ought you to be?"* Again, the Apostle Paul in 1 Thessalonians 4:16 said, *"For the Lord himself will come down from heaven, with a loud command, with the voice of the archangel and with the trumpet call of God, and the dead in Christ will rise first. After that, we who are still alive and are left will be caught up together with them in the clouds to meet the Lord in the air. And so we will be with the Lord forever."*

Are all the present-day predictions about the end of the world true? Are we indeed about to witness the end of creation as we know it? There are numerous interpretations about exactly how these events will unfold, but one thing every preacher and teacher who subscribes to this world view agree upon is that all these things will definitely occur during the "last days." The Bible also agrees. The real question is, are we living in the "last days"?

Understanding the Biblical time period known as the last days is critical to a proper interpretation of many confusing doctrines challenging the church today. In order to understand where we fit into God's plan we need to know the Scriptural time frame in

Jesus is Coming Soon?

which we are presently living. If we will allow it to do so, the Bible will answer all our questions about the last days.

We know from Scripture a lot of things were to happen during the "last days" leading up to the "great day of the Lord." Please take the time to look up each of these Scriptures and read them for yourself.

1. Israel would be ruled by foreigners. (Daniel 2:44, 7:25)
2. "Elijah" would come. (Malachi 4:5, Matthew 11:14)
3. The Messiah would be born in Bethlehem. (Daniel 9:25-27, Micah 5:2, John 7:42)
4. ALL prophecy would be fulfilled. (Luke 21:22)
5. The Holy Spirit would be poured out on all flesh. (Joel 2, Acts 2)
6. Miraculous signs and wonders would confirm the word. (Daniel 9:27, Mark 16:20, Acts 2, Acts 14:13, Hebrews 2:2-4)
7. The church would be established in Jerusalem. (Isaiah 2:1-3, Daniel 2:44, Acts 2)
8. The gospel would be preached to all the world, beginning at Jerusalem. (Daniel 9:27, Matthew 24:14, Mark 13:10)
9. The physical kingdom of Israel would be replaced by the true, spiritual kingdom. (Daniel 7-12, Matthew 24, Revelation 11:15)
10. Israel would reject the truth and the Messiah (Luke 9:22, 17:25)
11. Terrible times of suffering would exist, like nothing before or after. (Daniel 12:1, Matthew 24:19-22, Mark 13:17-19)

12. The Lord would come in judgment upon Israel and the nations. (Isaiah 66:15-16, Daniel 12:1-4, John 5:24-30, 12:31, Revelation 14:7)
13. The Lord would "shake the earth". (Isaiah 2:20-22, Haggai 2:6, Hebrews 12:25-28)
14. Armies would surround Jerusalem. (Daniel 12:9-12, Luke 21:20-21)
15. The temple would be desecrated. (Daniel 9:27, 11:31, 12:11, Matthew 24:15, Mark 13:14)
16. The dead would be raised. (Daniel 12:1-4, John 5:24-30)
17. Forgiveness of sins would finally be a reality. (Daniel 9:24, Joel 3, Hebrews 10:15-39)
18. The power of death would be forever destroyed. (Isaiah 28:17-19, Hosea 13:14, 1 Corinthians 15:55-57, Hebrews 2:13-15)
19. The city of Jerusalem and the physical temple would be totally destroyed. (Daniel 9:25-27, 11:16, Matthew 24:2, Mark 13:2, Luke 21:6, Revelation 18)
20. The New Jerusalem (spiritual nation of Israel, promised to Abraham) would be an everlasting kingdom. (Daniel 2:44-45, Hebrews 12:22-29, Revelation 21:1-5)
21. The dwelling of God would, once again, be with men. (Revelation 21:1-5)

Can we know for sure the historical time frame of these Biblical "last days"? **Yes!** The concept of "the last days" and the events that would happen during those times begin in Old Testament prophecies. This time period is first mentioned in Isaiah 2 where the Bible says, *"This is what Isaiah son of Amoz saw **concerning Judah and Jerusalem**: In the last days the mountain of the Lord's* *temple will be established...and all nations will stream to it."* Isaiah clearly identifies the "last days" with Judah and Jerusalem. A closer examination of the entire chapter reveals several significant things about those last days that we will see again and again as we study further.

First, he says it will be during these "last days" of Judah and Jerusalem that *"...the mountain of the Lord's temple will be established as chief among the mountains."* What is this mountain that the Lord will establish in these last days? We read in Exodus where God gave the Law of Moses and confirmed his covenant with the kingdom of Israel on Mt. Sinai. Mt. Sinai was often referred to in Old Testament Scriptures as the Holy Mountain or the Mountain of the Lord.

After David became king of Israel, he conquered a Jebusite fortress located on Mt. Zion and built a city around that area. It was called the City of David and later, Jerusalem. Zion came to designate the entire area of Jerusalem and later became a metonym for Solomon's temple, the city of Jerusalem, and the entire concept of God's presence among his people.

There are many Old Testament prophesies which foretold of the salvation of the Lord going out from Zion. In Zechariah 8:3, *"This is what the Lord says: 'I will return to Zion and dwell in Jerusalem. Then Jerusalem will be called the City of Truth, and the mountain of the Lord Almighty will be called the Holy Mountain.'"* We see from this, and a host of other Scriptures, that it was Zion, not Sinai, which would eventually represent the Holy Mountain of the Lord Almighty.

The writer of Hebrews makes this abundantly clear in chapter 12:18-29 when he compares the covenant that was represented by Sinai to the New Covenant in Jesus Christ represented by Mt. Zion. *"You have not come to a mountain* (Sinai) *that can be touched and that is burning with fire; to darkness, gloom and storm; to a trumpet blast or to such a voice speaking words that those who heard it begged that no further word be spoken to them, because they could not bear what was commanded: 'If even an animal touches the mountain, it must be stoned.' The sight was so terrifying that Moses said, 'I am trembling with fear.' But you have come to Mount Zion, to the heavenly Jerusalem, the city of the living God. You have come to thousands upon thousands of angels in joyful assembly, to the church of the firstborn, whose names are written in heaven. You have come to God, the judge of all men, to the spirits of righteous men made perfect, to Jesus the mediator of a new covenant, and to the sprinkled blood that speaks a better word than the blood of Abel."*

We can clearly understand from Scripture that the church (also figuratively called Mt. Zion, The Heavenly Jerusalem, The City of God) was the "mountain of the Lord's temple" that was to be established during the "last days" of Judah and Jerusalem. And we know Jesus lived and died during these same "last days," as did his apostles. We also know the church was established during these same "last days," and the word of the Lord went out from Jerusalem, just as Isaiah predicted.

We also see in the remainder of Isaiah 2 some additional things which the prophet saw would happen during the "last days of Judah and Jerusalem." Verses 12-17 say, *"The Lord has a day in store"* when *"...the arrogance of man will be brought low and the pride of men humbled; the Lord alone will be exalted in that day."* Verse 19 says, *"Men will flee to caves in the rocks and to holes in the ground from dread of the Lord and the splendor of his majesty, when he rises to shake the earth."*

These events are of particular interest because they are quoted by Jesus and other New Testament writers as the time of their fulfillment neared. One cannot understand Isaiah and apply the New Testament quotations of these same passages to some future ending of the universe. These were things that were to happen during the "last days" of Judah and Jerusalem. They have nothing to do with the end of the physical creation or the time in which we are living today.

God demonstrated for Hosea in chapter three how, just as he had been estranged from his wife Gomer and was now to be reconciled, Israel would also return to the Lord in their last days. *"For the Israelites will live many days without king or prince, without sacrifice or sacred stones, without ephod or idol. Afterward the Israelites will return and seek the Lord their God and David their king. They will come trembling to the Lord and to his blessings in the last days"* (Hosea 3:4-5). These "last days" are the same as Isaiah's...the last days of Israel...not the last days of the physical earth.

A third description of the "last days" comes from Micah 4. The end of chapter three says, *"...Zion will be plowed like a field, and Jerusalem will become a heap of rubble, the temple hill a mound overgrown with thickets."* He follows this description of Jerusalem's destruction with, *"In the last days the mountain of the Lord's temple will be established...and people will stream to it."* Again, nobody can understand these prophetic "last days" to be anything other than the last days of Judah and Jerusalem, or the physical nation of Israel.

That the "last days" do not pertain to the present is also logical. The physical nation of Israel was God's prototype of the church. She had a specific purpose and time and would be replaced by the "true kingdom" identified in Scripture as the church. The kingdom of Israel indeed had "last days" and came to an end in A.D. 70. The kingdom of God has NO END, therefore, can have no last days. The term "last days" cannot apply to the church, or the "church dispensation," since, according to the Bible, it will never end.

One of the clearest and easiest to understand books of prophecy concerning the "end times" is the book of Joel. Although Joel did not specifically use the phrase, "the last days,"

Peter, referring to his prophecy, did. In Acts 2, speaking of the strange events that were happening on the day of Pentecost, Peter said, *"This is that which was spoken by the prophet Joel;* **in the last days** *God will pour out his Spirit..."* Peter had no doubt that what was happening was the fulfillment of prophecies concerning the "last days of Israel" spoken of by Joel (Acts 2:17-21). Old Testament prophecies continually contrasted the physical nation of Israel, which would be destroyed, with the eternal kingdom that was Israel's true inheritance. The "world" of the Jews (physical Israel) would be destroyed, have "last days," "end times," and would one day cease to exist.

To understand the teachings in the New Testament concerning the "last days," the "day of the Lord," and the "time of the end," one must consider that these events all came from the Old Testament prophesies and the first-century writers used the same language and imagery as was used by the prophets. In Isaiah 13 there is a prophecy against Babylon (vs. 1). Verse 4 says, *"The Lord Almighty is mustering an army of war."* Verse 6 says, *"Wail for the day of the Lord is near; it will come like destruction from the Almighty."* In verses 10 and 13 we read, *"The stars of heaven and their constellations will not show their light. The rising sun will be darkened and the moon will not give its light...Therefore I will make the heavens tremble; and the earth will shake from its place at the wrath of the Lord Almighty, in the day of his burning anger."* Verses 17-19 tell how God is going to accomplish this. *"See, I will stir up the Medes...Babylon, the jewel of kingdoms, the glory of the Babylonians pride, will be overthrown by God like Sodom and Gomorrah."*

The Medes did overthrow the Babylonian Empire just as Isaiah predicted. Isaiah was speaking of the end of the Babylonian kingdom, not the end of the world. This apocalyptic language is typical throughout the Old Testament prophesies concerning God's judgment against nations. Descriptive terms like the day of the Lord, the coming of the Lord, the heavens and earth being destroyed, the stars falling, the sun and moon turning to blood or not giving their light...all these were used dozens of times throughout the prophesies and in every case were describing God's coming judgment on one or more nations. It should not surprise anyone with knowledge of Old Testament Scriptures to find this same language used to describe the destruction of Jerusalem and its temple and the end of the kingdom of Israel. Neither the Old nor New Testament Scriptures ever speak of the destruction of the universe and the end of time as taught by many today.

As we examine the New Testament passages which refer to the "last days," we quickly see they refer to the same time frame originally defined by the prophets. Hebrews begins, *"In the past God spoke to our forefathers through the prophets at many times and in various ways,* **but in these last days** *he has spoken to us by his Son..."* Jesus lived, taught, and died during the "last days" of Israel. Since the church was not established until after his death and resurrection, the "last days" could not refer to the present time often referred to as the "church dispensation." And to apply the term in this passage to the end of the universe makes absolutely no sense at all. Jesus spoke during Isaiah's "last days of Judah and Jerusalem." The Hebrew writer knew the Old Testament Scriptures.

In 2 Timothy 3:1-5, Paul wrote of *"...terrible times in the last days."* These were the same "last days" and "terrible times" spoken of by Daniel and Isaiah. Paul was not making up some new "last days" which have no Scriptural basis. He was speaking of the same time Jesus discussed in Matthew 24 when he quoted from Daniel stating that *"...there would be terrible times unequaled from the beginning of the world until now...and never to be equaled again."* Jesus, in Matthew 24, was speaking of the destruction of Jerusalem. In Luke's vivid description of these same events for the Gentile audience he said, *"When you see Jerusalem surrounded by*

The Last Days

armies, you will know that its desolation is near. Then let those who are in Judea flee to the mountains, let those in the city get out, and let those in the country not enter the city. **For this is the time of punishment in fulfillment of all that has been written**" (Luke 21:20-22).

Peter also spoke of the "last days" in his writings. In 1 Peter 1:20 he said, *"He* (Jesus) *was chosen before the creation of the world, but was revealed in* **these last times** *for your sake."* Jesus was revealed (born) in the "last days" of Israel, not the last days of the physical universe. Again in 2 Peter 3 he said, *"I want you to recall the words spoken in the past by the holy prophets and the command given by our Lord and Savior through your apostles. First of all, you must understand that in* **the last days** *scoffers will come...they will say 'where is this coming he promised?'* " Comparing this passage with the "holy prophets" and the words spoken by Jesus in Matthew, Mark, and Luke describing these very times, Peter's message is clear. He was speaking of the exact same "last days" as all the rest. He could not have been speaking of different "last days" unless one can find them in the "holy prophets" and in the words of Jesus.

Jude 18 mentioned the same thing as did Peter when he said, *"...remember what the apostles of our Lord Jesus Christ foretold. They said to you, 'in* **the last times** *there will be scoffers who will follow their own ungodly desires'* " Again, Jude was discussing the same "last times" as everyone else in Scripture. Peter had to deal with some of these scoffers in 2 Peter 3.

Finally, the Apostle John in 1 John 2:18 said, *"Dear children, this is* **the last hour;** *and as you have heard that the antichrist is coming, even now many antichrists have come. This is how we know it is the last hour..."* John clearly identifies the time in which he was living as the "last hour." Why are modern-day "prophets" still predicting some future coming of the "antichrists" when John clearly said they had already come in his day? He knew from Jesus' teachings they were coming in that generation and would precede the coming of the Son of Man. In Matthew 16:27-28 Jesus said, *"For the Son of Man is going to come in his Father's glory with his angels, and then he will reward each person according to what he has done. I tell you the truth, some who are standing here will not taste death before they see the Son of Man coming in his kingdom."* In Matthew 24:30-35 and Luke 21:25-33, describing the events that would take place when the temple was destroyed, Jesus said, *"At that time they will see the Son of Man coming in a cloud with power and great glory. When these things begin to take place, stand up and lift up your heads, because your redemption is drawing near."* When would these things take place? In those same passages Jesus told them to watch for the signs and said, *"I tell you the truth, this generation will certainly not pass away until all these things have happened."* One of the many signs they were to watch for was false (anti) christs. John believed Jesus and was watching. He said they had come, which is how he knew it was the "last hour."

Some might contend that the last days began in the first century but will continue until the end of the world. Depending on the wording of a particular translation, there are statements in the Bible about the "end of the world." Like everything else, we must look at the Scriptures and let them explain what is being revealed. In Genesis 9:11 God told Noah, *"...neither shall there any more be a flood to destroy the earth."* We all know the earth (dirt) was not destroyed in the flood. The term "earth" was used to denote all living animals, including mankind.

The term "world" is used throughout Scripture to refer to a particular society, an age, a dispensation, etc. In Hebrews 9:26 the Scripture says, *"But now he (Christ) has appeared once for all at the end of the ages to do away with sin by the sacrifice of himself."* The King James Version renders this, *"But now once in the end of the world hath he appeared to put away sin by the sacrifice of himself."* In the New American Standard Version we find perhaps the best translation of the phrase, *"But now once at the consummation of the ages he has been manifested to put away sin by the sacrifice of Himself."* Young's Literal Translation says, *"At the full end of the ages."* Regardless of translation, the verse clearly says that Jesus appeared at the "end of the world." This is consistent with Jesus' own statement in Matthew 24:3 that he would come at the end of the age (world). And, citing examples from Israel's history, Paul explains in 1 Corinthians 10:11, *"These things happened to them as examples and were written down as warnings for us, on whom the fulfillment of the ages has come."* We know that the coming of the Messiah, his crucifixion as the ultimate Passover Lamb, his victory over death, and the establishment of the eternal kingdom (church) was the promised fulfillment of the ages. That happened, just as promised, during the "last days" of that age...the age or days (or world) of physical Israel.

In a careful examination of Scripture it becomes vividly apparent that one's understanding of the Biblical concept of the "last days" is paramount in properly interpreting the timing and events associated with the "coming of the Lord" and all other eschatological events. All the New Testament writers spoke of the fulfillment of the prophetical, Biblical "last days" of Judah and Jerusalem. There is not one single Scripture that speaks of some future "coming of Jesus" to destroy the physical creation. There are many other passages that have not been mentioned here...and some of them require diligent study. Even Peter said Paul wrote some things that were difficult to understand. Whatever we teach must be consistent with what we do understand, and we can know from Scripture that the "last days" were the last days of Israel.

Summary points:
1. The Bible defines the "last days" to be the last days of Israel.
2. Jesus and the apostles lived during the "last days" of Israel.

3. The church was established during the "last days" of Israel.
4. An eternal kingdom cannot have "last days."
5. The "abomination of desolation" that preceded the destruction of the Jerusalem temple was accompanied by terrible times in the "last days" that would never be equaled again.
6. Jerusalem and its temple were destroyed in A.D. 70 exactly as Jesus predicted.
7. Some people of that generation, including John, lived to see the "coming of the Son of Man" during the "last days."

Since we know from Daniel, Joel, and Jesus there would *be* "...*terrible times unequaled from the beginning of the world until now...and never to be equaled again,*" and from Jesus that the destruction of the temple would be this "...*time of punishment in fulfillment of all that has been written,*" the only way one can believe that a future "more terrible time" is still coming in the "last days" is to subscribe to the notion that we are still living in the "last days," dismiss the events of A.D. 70 as irrelevant, and the scoffers Peter wrote about were right...Jesus failed to do what he said he would do. He clearly said, *"This generation will certainly not pass away until all these things have happened"* (Matthew 24:34, Mark 13:30, Luke 21:32). In Matthew 16:27-28 Jesus also said, *"For the Son of Man is going to come in his Father's glory with his angels, and then he will reward each person according to what he has done. I tell you the truth, some who are standing here will not taste death before they see the Son of Man coming in his kingdom."* The scoffers of Peter's day, and the doomsday prophets of today, were and are wrong.

Some people object to the destruction of Jerusalem being the fulfillment of Daniel's and Jesus' prophesies by questioning whether that event could have possibly been the worst calamity to ever occur on earth, past, present or future. Would not the flood of Noah's day been more devastating since there were only eight people left on the earth? And even applied to the Jewish world, did not the holocaust of WW2 claim far more lives than the Roman invasion of Jerusalem in A.D. 70?

While it may seem plausible, this objection fails to recognize the spiritual significance of what happened in A.D. 70. Daniel's prophecy, which Jesus quoted, specifically concerned the Jewish nation. The kingdom of Israel was not just another nation in the world. They were called by God to be his chosen people for the express purpose of bringing the Messiah into the world. They were a special people, a Holy Nation. No other kingdom in the world ever had, or ever will have, that distinction. When Jerusalem and its temple were destroyed, that Holy Nation was completely obliterated from the earth, never to exist again. Nothing in the history of the human race had, or ever will have, the same eternal implications as that one event. The only possible way for this prophecy to still be in our future would be for the kingdom of Israel to be reestablished as God's chosen people and the temple rebuilt. This would mean that Jesus was not the promised Messiah and Christianity is a false religion. The reestablishment of a Jewish state in 1948 did not reinstate their position with Almighty God as his chosen people. That distinction now belongs to the New Jerusalem, the church. Jesus was, and is, the Son of God, the promised Messiah.

It is vital to the mission of the church that we understand the times in which we are living. The current preoccupation with the end of the world has taken us off message and off our mission. Christians are confused, not knowing whether to "go into all the world" or "run to the hills"! If the modern futurist message is true, the latter is the advice of Jesus. If it is not, we have a mission before us and an exciting message the world is dying to hear! We are not living in the "last days."

CHAPTER 4

The End of the World

Is the world coming to an end? It may surprise you to learn there are many Scriptures that say it is not. Following the flood God told Noah in Genesis 8:21-22, *"Never again will I curse the ground because of humans, even though every inclination of the human heart is evil from childhood. And never again will I destroy all living creatures, as I have done."* He said very clearly that he will never destroy all living creatures again.

He made a covenant with Noah and his descendants in Genesis 9:11-16, *"And I will establish my covenant with you, neither shall all flesh be cut off any more by the waters of a flood; neither shall there any more be a flood to destroy the earth. And God said, 'This is the token of the covenant which I make between me and you and every living creature that is with you, for perpetual generations: I do set my bow in the cloud, and it shall be for a token of a covenant between me and the earth. And it shall come to pass, when I bring a cloud over the earth, that the bow shall be seen in the cloud: And I will remember my covenant, which is between me and you and every living creature of all flesh; and the waters shall no more become a flood to destroy all flesh. And the bow shall be in the cloud; and I will look upon it, that I may remember the everlasting covenant between God and every living creature of all flesh that is upon the earth.'"*

God's promise was to never again destroy all living creatures. Because the flood was the method by which all living creatures were destroyed, when he made the covenant he chose a rainbow as a sign of the covenant. Because this second recording of God's promise specifically mentions the flood, there are religious teachers who claim God never promised that the earth would not be destroyed...just that it would not be destroyed **by water**. And they go on to say, misquoting what the Apostle Peter taught in 2 Peter 3, the next time God destroys the earth, he will use fire.

That is simply not the case. The promise was clear. *"Never again will I destroy all living creatures, as I have done."* The covenant, with the rainbow as its sign, was an **everlasting** covenant. If one believes what God promised Noah and sealed with a covenant, he will never again bring destruction upon the earth to destroy all living things. The water of the flood was not the object of God's promise...it was the annihilation of all living things.

Other Scriptures also say that the earth will not come to an end:

> Ecclesiastes 1:4 *"Generations come and generations go, but the earth remains forever."*
>
> Psalm 78:69 *"He built his sanctuary like the heights, like the earth that he established forever."*
>
> Psalm 104:5 *"He set the earth on its foundations; it can never be moved."*

Admittedly, there are also some passages of Scripture that, on the surface, appear to say the earth will come to an end. Further study may help shed some light on these passages. Remember, the Bible says the world was destroyed by the flood in Noah's day. Of course we realize it was not the physical earth that was destroyed, but the people and animals that lived on the earth. The term "world" is often used to refer to civilization in general or a specific historical time period, not the planet.

Let us examine some other time-related concepts that are sometimes confusing. There are three different "heavens and earth" discussed in Scripture. There are also different "worlds" or "ages." To understand whether or not the world is coming to an end, we need to first understand these very different creations, worlds, and ages.

The first heaven and earth is obviously recorded in Genesis 1:1, *"In the beginning God created the heavens and the earth."* This was the creation of the physical universe. The Bible, in a few instances, refers to the physical creation as the world. The Apostle Paul in Romans 1:20 wrote, *"For since the creation of the world God's invisible qualities—his eternal power and divine nature—have been clearly seen, being understood from what has been made, so that men are without excuse."* However, most references in the Bible to the world (often translated "age") refer either to the human population at a given time or a specific nation of people; not the physical creation.

In Genesis 11:1 the text reads, *"Now the whole world had one language and a common speech."* This was prior to God's confusing the people with multiple languages at the building of the tower of Babel so they would scatter out into other regions of the planet. In the Gospel of John 1:29, when Jesus was coming to John the Baptist to be baptized, John said, *"Look, the Lamb of God, who takes away the sin of the world!"* In both of these instances the Bible is obviously referring to the people of the world, not the planet.

The differing uses of the terms "world" and "age" are familiar to most people today since we use the same terminology in our own language. It is also important to understand that in the ancient Hebrew language in which the Old Testament was written, the term "heavens and earth" was used in exactly the same way. A close examination of Isaiah 51 clearly illustrates this.

In this passage the prophet is exhorting Israel to be faithful to God who not only created the heavens and earth (physical universe) but also created *their* heavens and earth (kingdom of Israel). In Isaiah 51:13 he says, *"And you forget the Lord your Maker, who stretched out the heavens and laid the foundations of the earth..."* In this verse the prophet is referring to the physical creation of the universe. Then in verses 15-16 he says, *"But I am the Lord your God, who divided the sea whose waves roared— The Lord of hosts is his name. And I have put My words in your mouth; I have covered you with the shadow of My hand, that I may plant the heavens, lay the foundations of the earth, and say to Zion, 'You are My people' "* (NKJV). In these verses he is speaking of how God brought them out of Egypt through the Red Sea so he could establish them as his own people. This establishment of the nation of Israel as God's people, his kingdom, was called "planting the heavens" and "laying the foundations of the earth." Since he refers to this "heavens and earth" as **Zion** and **My people**, we know for sure he was talking about creating a kingdom, not a physical universe. Do not forget, as we move forward into our study, that the physical creation is called the "heavens and earth" and the kingdom of Israel is also referred to in Scripture as the "heavens and earth." We should not be surprised to see later in Scripture the destruction of that kingdom described as the destruction of the "heavens and earth."

So far we see, in addition to the creation of the physical universe, there was a world (heavens and earth) age prior to the flood, which was destroyed by that event. We also see another world (heavens and earth) age of the kingdom of Israel, which came into being following the flood and was still in existence when Jesus and his apostles lived and taught. This is the "present age" referred to in the New Testament. In 1 Corinthians 2:8 the Apostle Paul, speaking of the gospel of Christ said, *"None of the rulers of this age understood it, for if they had, they would not have crucified the Lord of glory."* It was the rulers of "this age" (the Jews) who crucified Jesus.

This age in which Jesus and the apostles lived was going to end. In Matthew 24, Mark 13 and Luke 21 Jesus explained that Jerusalem and its temple would soon be destroyed. In Matthew 24:3 the disciples asked Jesus about this coming event. *"As Jesus* was sitting on the Mount of Olives, the disciples came to him privately. 'Tell us,' they said, 'when will this happen, and what will be the sign of your coming and of the end of the age?'" The end of the Jewish age did coincide with the destruction of the temple and we know from history this prophecy was fulfilled in A.D. 70.

But there was also an "age to come." This coming age would also see the creation of a "new heaven and earth." As Isaiah 65:17-18 foretold, *"Behold, I will create new heavens and a new earth. The former things will not be remembered, nor will they come to mind. But be glad and rejoice forever in what I will create, for I will create Jerusalem to be a delight and its people a joy."* Again, following a description of God's judgment on the nation, he promises in Isaiah 66:22, *"As the new heavens and the new earth that I make will endure before me, declares the Lord, so will your name and descendants endure."* The present "heavens and earth" would end but the new "heavens and earth" would never end.

And the Hebrew writer tells us this prophecy would be fulfilled in the church. In Hebrews 12:22-24 he says, *"But you have come to Mount Zion, to the heavenly Jerusalem, the city of the living God. You have come to thousands upon thousands of angels in joyful assembly, to the church of the firstborn, whose names are written in heaven. You have come to God, the judge of all men, to the spirits of righteous men made perfect, to Jesus the mediator of a new covenant, and to the sprinkled blood that speaks a better word than the blood of Abel."* And in Revelation 21:1, *"Then I saw a new heaven and a new earth, for the first heaven and the first earth had passed away, and there was no longer any sea."* The first heaven and earth was the physical nation or kingdom of Israel which was a prototype of the new heaven and earth, the spiritual kingdom of God, the church.

All the New Testament writers taught and wrote about the coming destruction of the "world" of the Jews. It was important because Jesus had explained to them how that event would fulfill Old Testament prophesies and bring to fruition the kingdom of heaven. However, many religious teachers today are confusing the teachings of Jesus and his disciples with a concept of the end of the physical universe which is not supported by Scripture.

One of the primary passages used to support this future, world-ending philosophy is 2 Peter 3:10-13, *"But the day of the Lord will come like a thief. The heavens will disappear with a roar; the elements will be destroyed by fire, and the earth and everything in it will be laid bare. Since everything will be destroyed in this way, what kind of people ought you to be? You ought to live holy and godly lives as you look forward to the day of God and speed its coming. That day will bring about the destruction of the heavens by fire, and the elements will melt in the heat. But in keeping with his promise we are looking forward to a new heaven and a new earth, the home of righteousness."* Out of context, these verses seem to support the idea that the earth will one day be destroyed by fire. Taken in its entire context, Peter's writings become clear.

Before Jesus left his apostles and ascended back into heaven he promised the Holy Spirit would come to guide them. In John 16:12-14 he told them, *"I have much more to say to you, more than you can now bear. But when he, the Spirit of truth, comes, he will guide you into all truth. He will not speak on his own; he will speak only what he hears, and he will tell you what is yet to come. He will bring glory to me by taking from what is mine and making it known to you."* The Holy Spirit's role in the lives of these early disciples was to help them remember what Jesus had taught and continue to reveal God's will to them, **including things that were yet to happen**, so they could write it down for our benefit.

Peter was keenly aware of the importance of the Holy Spirit's guidance in God's revelation. In 1 Peter 1:20 he said, *"Above all, you must understand that no prophecy of Scripture came about by the prophet's own interpretation. For prophecy never had its origin in the will of man, but men spoke from God as they were carried along by the Holy Spirit."* Peter was one of those men from God who would speak and write as he was guided by the Holy Spirit.

In his first letter, following his usual salutation, he began to explain some things about salvation that may seem a bit strange. He said in verse 3-4, *"Praise be to the God and Father of our Lord Jesus Christ! In his great mercy he has given us new birth into a living hope through the resurrection of Jesus Christ from the dead, and into an inheritance that can never perish, spoil or fade—kept in heaven for you, who through faith are shielded by God's power until the coming of the salvation that is ready to be revealed in the last time."* Here the apostle was writing many years after the death, burial, and resurrection of Jesus speaking of the **coming of the salvation that is** (not was) **ready to be revealed in the last time.** What was there about salvation that was still to be revealed? To what time period was he referring when he said "the last time"? Remember this was the same apostle who preached the first gospel sermon on the day of Pentecost. In that sermon he was the one who identified these times as the ones spoken of by the prophet Joel when he said, *"In the last days God will pour out his Spirit…"*

Throughout the New Testament letters there is expressed time after time the concept of salvation being present, yet still coming. In Hebrews 12:28 the writer said, *"…we are receiving a kingdom."* Jesus' death on the cross was the sacrifice for our sin. His blood was shed for our atonement, which made possible our salvation. The sacrificial lamb had been slain. But there was more to come.

Continuing in 2 Peter verse 10, *"Concerning this salvation, the prophets, who spoke of the grace that was to come to you, searched intently and with the greatest care, trying to find out the time and circumstances to which the Spirit of Christ in them was pointing when he predicted the sufferings of Christ and the glories that would follow."* Not only did the prophets predict the sufferings of Christ, but also the **"…glories that would follow."** There must have been more to these "last days" than the crucifixion of Jesus. Peter also understood the consummation of the ages. He knew Jesus had been sacrificed for the sins of the world. He was at the trial. He also knew, by divine guidance of the Holy Spirit, that there was more to be accomplished. Peter knew the ritual the High Priest went through in sacrificing blood for sin. He had taken many animals to the priest and waited anxiously for his emergence from the Holy of Holies to know his sacrifice was accepted by God.

In 1 Peter 4:7 he said, *"The end of all things is near. Therefore be clear minded and self-controlled so that you can pray."* Is it even remotely logical that he was speaking of the end of the physical universe? If so, Peter and the other New Testament writers were sadly misguided by the Holy Spirit in regard to the timing. Are we still waiting for salvation to be revealed? In keeping with what Jesus and Scripture says on the subject, salvation was to be completely revealed in the last days of Israel. Once all the things the prophets had foretold and Jesus said would have to happen were fulfilled, the atonement would be complete and our Great High Priest would appear signifying not only God's acceptance of his blood for our sins, but the end of the Old Covenant. Then the physical temple would be forever removed from the earth. This was the "end of all things" necessary to complete God's wonderful mystery of salvation. A few of these things were still to be revealed at the time of Peter's writing. If they have not yet happened, our salvation is not yet complete. (The atonement ritual performed annually by the High Priest will be discussed in greater detail in the next chapter.)

In his second letter, Peter continued with a much more detailed account of these final things that remained to be revealed concerning this salvation. In 2 Peter 3:1-2 he said, *"Dear friends, this is now my second letter to you. I have written both of them as reminders to stimulate you to wholesome thinking. I want you to recall the words spoken in the past by the holy prophets and the command given by our Lord and Savior through your apostles."* He said he had written both of his letters to remind his readers of what the prophets said and what Jesus taught.

Peter began this chapter telling them what he was saying was nothing new. It could be found in the Old Testament prophecies and in the teachings of Jesus. In verse 3-4 he said, *"First of all, you must understand that in the last days scoffers will come, scoffing and following their own evil desires. They will say, 'Where is this 'coming' he promised? Ever since our fathers died, everything goes on as it has since the beginning of creation.'"*

Who had predicted scoffers and false teachers? Jesus. These people were now taunting the first century Christians with Jesus' own words. *"Where is this 'coming' he promised?"* Everyone understood exactly what Jesus had said, that this generation would not pass away until all these things happened. They were some thirty years beyond the death of Jesus and it had not happened. Jesus must have been a fake.

Peter began to answer their argument with a comparison to the days of Noah. Verses 5-6, *"But they deliberately forget that long ago by God's word the heavens existed and the earth was formed out of water and by water. By these waters also the world of that time was deluged and destroyed."* No doubt there were a lot of people in Noah's time who did not believe the world was going to be destroyed, but they were wrong. God did exactly what he said he would do. Notice Peter said the *"...world of that time was destroyed."* He was now telling them the "world of this time" is about to be destroyed. Since the destruction of the world during the time of Noah did not result in the end of the physical creation, why would anyone think the coming destruction of the world in Peter's letter would be any different?

Peter repeated precisely what Jesus had taught in verse 7, *"By the same word the present heavens and earth* (world) *are reserved for fire, being kept for the day of judgment and destruction of ungodly men."* In Matthew 25:31-33 Jesus had said, *"When the Son of Man comes in his glory, and all the angels with him, he will sit on his throne in heavenly glory. All the nations will be gathered before him, and he will separate the people one from another as a shepherd separates the sheep from the goats. He will put the sheep on his right and the goats on his left."* Jesus continued, *"Then he will say to those on his left, 'Depart from me, you who are cursed, into the eternal fire prepared for the devil and his angels"* (vs. 41).

In one of the most misunderstood and misapplied verses in the Bible, Peter explained to them why they should not listen to the scoffers. In verse 8 he said, *"But do not forget this one thing, dear friends: With the Lord a day is like a thousand years, and a thousand years are like a day. The Lord is not slow in keeping his promise, as some understand slowness. He is patient with you, not wanting anyone to perish, but everyone to come to repentance."*

Many Christians today have been taught that one cannot take God literally when he makes a statement about time because God doesn't keep time like we do. A day is like a thousand years to God, so when God says he will do something in forty years, he may mean forty thousand years. And, in this case, when Jesus said all these things will happen in this generation, he may have meant a thousand generations. This is utter nonsense and is the complete opposite of what Peter was saying.

As was previously discussed in the first chapter, when God makes an explicit time statement, he means it and he keeps it. When he told the Israelites they would have to wander in the desert for forty years, he meant exactly forty years. And forty years **to the day** they crossed over the Jordan into the Promised Land. When God said forty years, he did not mean some undetermined amount of time.

God is not slow keeping his promise! He never has been, he never will be, and he wasn't in the days of Peter. Peter's message to the first century Christians was clear. God can remember a thousand years as easily as he can remember one day. God does not forget over time, nor does he forget what he says about time. He had not forgotten Jesus' promise. He said he would come in their generation…HE DID!

Then Peter proceeded to explain how the end would come and again chose the same terminology used by Jesus. 2 Peter 3:10-13,

> "But the day of the Lord will come like a thief. The heavens will disappear with a roar; the elements will be destroyed by fire, and the earth and everything in it will be laid bare. Since everything will be destroyed in this way, what kind of people ought you to be? You ought to live holy and godly lives as you look forward to the day of God and speed its coming. That day will bring about the destruction of the heavens by fire, and the elements will melt in the heat. But in keeping with his promise we are looking forward to a new heaven and a new earth, the home of righteousness."

Peter used the Greek word "ouranos" which is translated "heavens" to denote that which would be destroyed. This is the same term Jesus used in Matthew 24:33 when he said, *"Heaven and earth will pass away…"* Had either of them meant the physical universe, they would have used the word "kosmos." It is the same terminology from the prophecy of Isaiah 67:17, speaking of the time when the physical nation of Israel would find her ultimate fulfillment in the eternal kingdom. The prophet said, *"Behold, I will create new heavens and a new earth. The former things will not be remembered, nor will they come to mind."* The Scriptures contain numerous similar passages referring to the old kingdom of Israel as a world that would pass away, replaced by a "new heaven and earth." Remember that Peter said he would bring to mind the things spoken by the prophets and what Jesus had taught. This is one more example of just that.

He also said the *"...elements will melt in the heat."* The word "elements" is the Greek word "stoicheion" and appears seven times in the New Testament. Twice in Galatians (4:3 & 9) and twice in Colossians (2:8 & 20) it refers to the basic principles of this world to which we die when we become Christians. Once in Hebrews 5:12 it refers to the elementary truths of God's word. The other two times the word is used is here in 2 Peter 3:10 & 12. The word means the principles upon which a society is built. It refers here to the basic principles or "elements" of that world which was passing away, the world of physical Israel, the Jewish world. Never does this word refer to trees and dirt. There is nothing in these verses that teach the physical universe would be destroyed. Actually the opposite is true. The universe was going to undergo a "consummation" or changing of the ages. Something imperfect (physical Israel) was going to be destroyed and the perfect spiritual kingdom would replace it, which is exactly what happened. What a blessing that was to the cosmos!

Also notice Peter said, *"But in keeping with his promise we are looking forward to a new heaven and a new earth, the home of righteousness."* This new heaven and new earth was to follow the destruction of the heavens by fire and the elements melting in the heat. The New Testament is abundantly clear that the "new heaven and earth, the home of the righteous" is the spiritual kingdom of heaven, the church. So, if the old "heaven and earth" has not yet been destroyed, the new kingdom of heaven has not yet been established. That means the church will not exist until after the world ends. Jesus came to build his church. He did not fail in his mission.

No wonder Peter's next comment in 2 Peter 3:14 was, *"So then, dear friends, since you are looking forward to this, make every effort to be found spotless, blameless and at peace with him."* It is difficult to see how a cataclysmic destruction of the universe would be something to look forward to, but the revealing of God's salvation and the establishment of his eternal spiritual kingdom…now that was something to be excited about!

Before leaving this subject Peter had some interesting words to say about the Apostle Paul's writings and those who would distort the teachings about these matters. In verses 15-16 he said, *"Bear in mind that our Lord's patience means salvation, just as our dear brother Paul also wrote you with the wisdom that God gave him. He writes the same way in all his letters, speaking in them of these matters. His letters contain some things that are hard to understand, which ignorant and unstable people distort, as they do the other Scriptures, to their own destruction."*

The Apostle Paul wrote two short letters to the church in Thessalonica. He began the first by complementing them on their faith that was well known in the region. He said the churches in Macedonia and Achaia had given glowing reports of their understanding of Scripture. In 1 Thessalonians 1:8-10 he said, *"Therefore we do not need to say anything about it, for they themselves report what kind of reception you gave us. They tell how you turned to God from idols to serve the living and true God, and to wait for his Son from heaven, whom he raised from the dead—Jesus, who rescues us from the coming wrath."* Paul was speaking of the same coming Jesus predicted and the same time of wrath that was to have greater consequences than anything that had ever happened before or would ever happen again.

We learn in chapter 4:13-18 of their concern about those faithful disciples who had died before the coming of the Lord. What would happen to them? Paul said, *"Brothers, we do not want you to be ignorant about those who fall asleep, or to grieve like the rest of men, who have no hope. We believe that Jesus died and rose again and so we believe that God will bring with Jesus those who have fallen asleep in him. According to the Lord's own word, we tell you that we who are still alive, who are left till the coming of the Lord, will certainly not precede those who have fallen asleep."* Jesus had said earlier to the disciples, *"I tell you the truth, some who are standing here will not taste death before they see the kingdom of God come with power"* (Mark 9:1, Luke 9:27). Paul knew some Christians to whom he was writing would be *"...left till the coming of the Lord"* and live to see these events unfold.

Verse 16 continues, *"For the Lord himself will come down from heaven, with a loud command, with the voice of the archangel and with the trumpet call of God, and the dead in Christ will rise first."* This is the same coming that Jesus said would happen before that generation passed.

Then Paul explained what would happen to those who live beyond those last days. *"After that, we who are still alive and are left will be caught up together with them in the clouds to meet the Lord in the air. And so we will be with the Lord forever. Therefore encourage each other with these words"* (vs. 17-18). The Greek word (EPEITA) translated "after that" in the NIV, or "then" in some other translations, is used when speaking only of things in sequence. It is sometimes translated "thereafter" or "thereupon" or "afterward." It literally means what happens "after" some other event has occurred.

Paul did not say all those who remain would be immediately caught up to heaven in a worldwide "rapture." The question he was answering was what happens when people die. His answer was simple. Those who died prior to the coming of the Lord would be raised and be with him at that time. Those who are still living and die "after that" event will actually never die. When they experience physical death, they will simply be caught up to be with the Lord and join all those who have gone on before. That is exactly what Jesus said in John 11:26, *"...and whoever lives and believes in me* **will never die***. Do you believe this?"*

Remember, in the context of redemption, Scripture is always speaking of spiritual death and spiritual life. Death has been destroyed. We will still leave our physical body one day. But we have eternal life, resurrection life, NOW. We will never again be separated from God. We will never die.

Having answered the question about what happens to dead people, Paul turned his attention to the coming day of the Lord. Paul used the same analogy Jesus did about this day coming like a thief in the night. Jesus specifically said they would not know the exact day and hour. However, both Jesus and Paul said it should not surprise believers because there was a whole litany of signs for which they should be watching. Paul said in Chapter 5:4-11, *"But you, brothers, are not in darkness so that this day should surprise you like a thief. You are all sons of the light and sons of the day…for God did not appoint us to suffer wrath but to receive salvation through our Lord Jesus Christ. Therefore encourage one another and build each other up, just as in fact you are doing."* Jesus and Paul both explained that those who were watching for the signs would not be surprised at the coming of the Lord.

In his second letter to the church in Thessalonica Paul continued to encourage them to remain faithful and watchful for the Lord's coming. We read in 2 Thessalonians 1:6-10, *"This will happen when the Lord Jesus is revealed from heaven in blazing fire with his powerful angels. He will punish those who do not know God and do not obey the gospel of our Lord Jesus. They will be punished with everlasting destruction and shut out from the presence of the Lord and from the majesty of his power on the day he comes to be glorified in his holy people and to be marveled at among all those who have believed. This includes you, because you believed our testimony to you."* Paul did not change the subject to some other coming. Earlier he told them not to worry about Christians who had died, or who would live beyond this time. Here he described the fate of those who had refused to believe and obey the gospel and accept the atonement sacrifice of the Lamb of God who could have taken away their sin. Just as the blessings of eternal life with Jesus await the saved, all who will ever live and refuse to obey the gospel have but one destiny. They will be punished with everlasting destruction and shut out from the presence of the Lord, which is spiritual death.

As in every generation since, there were those in the first century who misunderstood the teaching of Jesus concerning his second coming and the day of the Lord. There were scoffers who had decided that, because it had been almost three decades since Jesus was crucified and he had not yet returned and destroyed the temple and its worship as he said he would, he must have been a false prophet. The Apostle Peter explained to the early Christians that God neither forgets nor fails to keep a promise, but would indeed come in that generation (2 Peter 3). There were others who were saying the day of the Lord had come and the resurrection of the dead had already taken place. Paul addressed this false doctrine in 2 Thessalonians 2:1-12:

> *"Concerning the coming of our Lord Jesus Christ and our being gathered to him, we ask you, brothers, not to become easily unsettled or alarmed by some prophecy, report or letter supposed to have come from us, saying that the day of the Lord has already come. Don't let anyone deceive you in any way, for that day will not come until the rebellion occurs and the man of lawlessness is revealed, the man doomed to destruction. He will oppose and will exalt himself over everything that is called God or is worshiped, so that he sets himself up in God's temple, proclaiming himself to be God.*

Paul identified two of these false teachers in 2 Timothy 2:17-18, *"Among them are Hymenaeus and Philetus, who have wandered away from the truth. They say that the resurrection has already taken place, and they destroy the faith of some."*

Jesus is Coming Soon?

If Jesus and the apostles actually taught the coming of the Lord and the resurrection was to be the end of the entire universe, how could anyone in the first century have been deceived into believing it had already happened? The fact that Paul addressed this as a serious concern obviously meant neither he nor any of the first century Christians held this view of the second coming and the resurrection of the dead. They all understood exactly what Jesus had said about these things happening during their generation. And, just as Jesus had said would happen, there were false teachers, some claiming to be the "returned Christ" and others attempting to capitalize on their own imaginary version of his coming. Sound familiar?

At the time of Paul's writing, the fulfillment of these last days had not yet come. The abomination of desolation set up in the temple was still a few years in their future. But it did come. It came before that generation passed away, just as Jesus said it would. Every writer of the New Testament is in total agreement on this subject. Some of it may be difficult to understand, especially for us Gentiles. But the second coming of Jesus Christ to affirm the completion of the atonement sacrifice, to fully establish the kingdom of heaven and completely destroy the temple is a consistent, fully understandable teaching of God's word. All we have to do is study and believe what the Bible actually says.

CHAPTER 5

The Atonement Sacrifice

Jesus was born to die. He came to be the true sacrifice for sin, replacing the need for the annual atonement sacrifices in the temple. As John declared, he was "the lamb of God who takes away the sins of the world." But he was so much more. Jesus also came to become our Great High Priest, replacing the old Levitical priesthood. He came to establish the kingdom of heaven, replacing the physical kingdom of Israel. He came to be crowned King of Kings and reign on David's throne forevermore. He came to bring a new covenant, fulfilling the old one and taking it out of the way. He literally came to change everything! And it did not all happen on the cross.

That is why there is so much in the New Testament about what the Apostle Paul called the "consummation of the ages" and this "time of the end" was referred to as an "age-changing" period. Why did Jesus put so much importance on the destruction of Jerusalem and its temple? Is it important for us to understand these things today? If we are to properly understand the times in which we are living and what the future holds for Christians and the world, we must know what changed and when. We need to understand there was a change from one age to another, from one world to another, from one kingdom to another, from one covenant to another, from one priesthood to another. And we especially need to understand the ritual of the atonement sacrifice.

Perhaps the best source of information regarding these age-changing events and their timing is the New Testament book of Hebrews. With the exception of the last chapter which contains

The Atonement Sacrifice

some final encouragements and greetings, the entire book is dedicated to explaining the consummation of the ages.

In the first three verses the author lays out the basis of what he is going to be teaching. Hebrews 1:1-3, *"In the past God spoke to our forefathers through the prophets at many times and in various ways, but in these last days he has spoken to us by his Son, whom he appointed heir of all things, and through whom he made the universe. The Son is the radiance of God's glory and the exact representation of his being, sustaining all things by his powerful word. After he had provided purification for sins, he sat down at the right hand of the Majesty in heaven."* He immediately identifies the "ages past" when God spoke through the prophets, the time in which he is living as "these last days," and the subject of his letter; Christ, the Son of God. As we will see, he will spend the remainder of the book comparing the Old Covenant of Moses with the New Covenant in Christ, the one that was ending with the one that was just beginning, the physical kingdom with the spiritual kingdom, the inferior one to the superior one.

In chapter two the writer urges his readers to pay careful attention to the gospel message they had heard, for if people were punished for disobeying the Old Testament teachings, how can we escape punishment if we ignore the message of salvation *"...which was first announced by the Lord, was confirmed to us by those who heard him. God also testified to it by signs, wonders and various miracles, and gifts of the Holy Spirit distributed according to his will"* (2:3-4). In verse 5 he says *"...it is not to angels that he (God) has subjected the world to come, about which we are speaking,"* but it is subjected to Christ. Please notice two things in this verse. First, the passage says the spiritual kingdom of Christ is the "world to come," and second, this "world to come" is the subject of the text. He then speaks of the preeminence of Christ, how he shared our humanity so that *"...by his death he might destroy him who holds the power of death—that is, the devil—and free those who all their lives were held in slavery by their fear of death"* (2:14-15). Jesus did this by making atonement for sin.

In chapters 3 and 4 the author admonishes his Jewish readers to *"...fix their eyes on Jesus"* because he is far superior to Moses and has become the "Great High Priest." The subject of Jesus as the Great High Priest introduces us to the means by which the consummation of the ages will be possible. This is the main theme of this letter...**atonement**. Only the High Priest could make atonement for the sins of the people. But the Jewish priests were sinners and could only offer the blood of bulls and goats, which could not actually atone for sin. It would take a better sacrifice to do that. Jesus was that better sacrifice.

The writer explains in chapters 5 and 7 how Jesus' priesthood was not based on genealogy as required by the Law of Moses. Rather he was appointed by God Himself, "after the order" or similar to Melchizedek. This was one of the "age-changing" events, a change in the priesthood. *"For when there is a change of the priesthood, there must also be a change of the law"* (7:12). The Law of Moses gave specific and detailed instructions about the appointment of priests, and especially the High Priest. These men had to be of the tribe of Levi, direct descendants of Aaron who served as Israel's first High Priest.

Outside the book of Hebrews, Melchizedek is mentioned only two times in the Bible (Genesis 14:18, Psalm 110:4). He lived during the time of Abraham over four hundred years before the Law was given to Moses on Mt. Sinai. We are not given many details of his life, but Melchizedek was chosen by God to serve as a priest and when Abraham met him, he gave him a tenth of all his possessions. Melchizedek's priesthood was not based on his genealogy, but solely upon God's divine selection and appointment.

Jesus was a descendant of the tribe of Judah, not Levi. Based on his genealogy he had no claim to the priesthood. Under the Law of Moses he could not have served as High Priest. This is why the Hebrew writer says his priesthood is after the order of Melchizedek, not Aaron. In Chapter 7:16 he says, *"(Jesus) has become a priest not on the basis of a regulation as to his ancestry but on the basis of the power of an indestructible life."*

Also in verse 12 we see another "age-changing" event was a change in the law. As he said, if there was a change in the priesthood there had to be a change in the law since the law required the High Priest to be a direct descendant of Aaron. *"The former regulation is set aside because it was weak and useless (for the law made nothing perfect), and a better hope is introduced, by which we draw near to God"* (7:18-19). Unlike the former priests under the Old Law, Jesus would remain the High Priest forever, and he could actually save people from their sins because of his superior sacrifice.

In the first part of chapter 8 we see this Great High Priest serves at a different sanctuary. The Old Levitical high priest served at a copy of God's sanctuary here on earth, which was first located in a "traveling tabernacle" built by the Israelites in the wilderness. This tabernacle had one room designated the Holy of Holies, which symbolized the place where God lived. Only the High Priest could enter the presence of God in the Holy of Holies once each year to offer the annual atonement sacrifice for sin. Once the Israelites moved into their promised land and the kingdom was established under King David, Jerusalem was selected as the permanent site of the tabernacle. Solomon built the temple to replace the original tent that had been used since the wilderness wanderings. It was in this temple the High Priests continued to serve. Jesus was not appointed High Priest under the Law of Moses. He did not enter the Holy of Holies in the temple in Jerusalem. He offered his blood sacrifice in the heavenly Holy of Holies before the very throne of God.

As we continue we see another "age-changing" event, a New Covenant. *"The time is coming, declares the Lord, when I will make a new covenant with the house of Israel and with the house of Judah. It will not be like the covenant I made with their forefathers when I took them by the hand to lead them out of Egypt...By calling this covenant 'new,' he has made the first one obsolete; and what is obsolete and aging will soon disappear"* (8:8-13).

The Old Covenant was passing away. The text clearly says *"...what is obsolete and aging will soon disappear."* It was not yet gone. Doesn't the Bible say the Old Law was "nailed to the cross"? Yes, in Colossians 2:14 Paul wrote, *"He forgave us all our sins, having canceled the written code, with its regulations, that was against us and that stood opposed to us; he took it away, nailing it to the cross."* Hebrews was written some thirty years after the crucifixion of Jesus. Why did it not say the Old Covenant had already disappeared? Because, as we shall soon see, the atonement work of Jesus was not finished. The cross was the fatal blow to the power of the Old Law. The perfect sacrifice of Jesus on the cross rendered it obsolete. But until the old Jewish system (world, heaven and earth) was destroyed, the law would remain.

Jesus said in Matthew 5:17-18, *"Do not think that I have come to abolish the Law or the Prophets; I have not come to abolish them but to fulfill them. I tell you the truth,* **until heaven and earth disappear***, not the smallest letter, not the least stroke of a pen, will by any means disappear from the Law until everything is accomplished."* In Isaiah 51 God told the Israelites he had led them out of Egypt across the Red Sea, given them his law, *"That I may plant the heavens, lay the foundations of the earth, and say to Zion, 'You are My people.'"* It was this "heaven and earth" (kingdom of Israel) to which Jesus referred when he said not the least part of the Law of Moses would disappear until "heaven and earth" had disappeared. The Law could not disappear until everything in it was fulfilled. Jesus said that is what he came to do.

The Atonement Sacrifice

Jesus' death on the cross was what made all of the "age-changing" events possible, but the actual changing of the ages did not occur on the day of his crucifixion. Nothing could change until the atonement sacrifice had been completed. Once that had happened there would indeed have been a change in the law and the priesthood. Then the Old Covenant, its temple and worship, would disappear. The atonement sacrifice was not complete with the slaying of the sacrificial lamb. The blood still had to be taken into the Holy of Holies and sprinkled on the Mercy Seat covering the Ark of the Covenant. Jesus' death was the beginning of this ritual, not the completion of it.

This may be the most critical point to understand concerning the "second coming" of Jesus. The Old Covenant was a prototype of the new one to be revealed during the "last days" of Israel. In the first covenant only the High Priest could enter the Holy of Holies, only to offer a blood sacrifice...first for his own sin, then for the sins of the people. This ritual is described in Leviticus 16 and required the High Priest to enter the Most Holy Place (and reappear) *twice*. There were actually two atonement sacrifices. The first time the High Priest entered with blood for himself. When he went behind the veil, he was entering (symbolically) into the presence of God, which was a place a sinful person could not enter and live. Since death was the consequence of sin, he was, in a very real sense, entering the "realm of death." If he entered the Most Holy Place without a blood sacrifice for his own sin, or if his sacrifice was not acceptable to God, he would die. His first appearance indicated to the people that he was acceptable to God as the High Priest to offer the sacrifice for the people.

He would then take a second amount of blood from their offering, return behind the veil, and make the sacrifice for the sins of the people. They anxiously waited for his second appearing, proving that God had accepted this blood for their sins. Only then were they assured of their atonement and could know they were justified before God for one more year. Please note that the atonement sacrifice was not complete with the death of the sacrificial lamb. To make atonement the High Priest, after the lamb was killed outside the temple, had to take some of the blood into the Holy of Holies, into the presence of God, to make the atonement for sin.

Jesus became the High Priest of the New Covenant. The ritual was exactly the same as under the Old Covenant...only the sacrifice was better. His perfect blood was the permanent remedy for sin. But he had to go through the same exercise as every previous High Priest. On the cross he shed his own blood that would be used for the atonement for sin. However, when Jesus died he did not enter the realm of death with a sin offering. As a matter of fact, technically his blood was not actually spilled until after he was dead. He entered death with NO sacrifice for Himself. This was the ultimate test of his complete lack of sin. This was equivalent to the High Priest walking into the Holy of Holies with NO blood offering.

The Bible teaches that Jesus had no sin. Anyone can make that claim. It was his resurrection from the grave that absolutely proved him to have been sinless. Had Jesus had even one sin, he would still be dead and would have never returned. The Apostle Paul said it was his resurrection that God used to declare that he was who he claimed to be, the Son of God. Paul says of Jesus, "...*who through the Spirit of holiness was declared with power to be the Son of God by his resurrection from the dead: Jesus Christ our Lord*" (Romans 1:3-5). And in Hebrews 7:16 it says, "*(Jesus) has become a priest not on the basis of a regulation as to his ancestry but on the basis of the power of an indestructible life.*" In verses 27-28 of that same chapter we read, "*Unlike the other high priests, he does not need to offer sacrifices day after day, first for his own sins, and then for the sins of the people. He sacrificed for their sins once for all when he offered himself. For the law appoints as high priests men in all their weakness; but the oath,*

The Atonement Sacrifice

which came after the law, appointed the Son, who has been made perfect forever."

The most important ritual God ever gave was the atonement, and Jesus had to complete all of it. Anybody could have claimed to be the Messiah, and even claimed to be sinless. His appearing from the grave was absolutely necessary to establish not only his High Priesthood, but that no additional sacrifices were needed. He had truly overcome death! His first appearing (bodily resurrection) proved that God had accepted him as the Great High Priest for the people. But Jesus still had to take his blood, go into the heavenly Holy of Holies, and fulfill the sacrifice for the sins of the people. By doing this he became *"...the lamb of God who takes away the sins of the world"* (John 1:29). To finish the second and final part of the atonement ritual, he had to go away again, after he had appeared the first time from the grave, into the Holy of Holies to take his blood as the atonement for our sins. This is why he explained to Mary at the tomb she could not "hold onto him" now because he had to return to the Father.

So after Jesus had been seen by a sufficient number of people to prove beyond any doubt that he was alive and accepted as God's High Priest, he left this earth to make the final sacrifice in the Most Holy Place. Hebrews 9:24 says, *"For Christ did not enter a man-made sanctuary that was only a copy of the true one; he entered heaven itself, now to appear for us in God's presence."* The eager anticipation of his "second coming" that we read about in the New Testament was because they understood the significance and the details of the atonement. His return would announce to the world that the sacrifice had been accepted by God and that the people were forgiven!

This same writer in Hebrews 9:28 said, *"Christ was sacrificed once to take away the sins of many people; and* **he will appear a second time***, not to bear sin, but* **to bring salvation to those who are waiting for him***.*" It was in view of the completion of the atonement sacrifice for sin that Jesus taught that his coming would complete our redemption. In Luke 21:27-28, speaking of the destruction of Jerusalem and its temple, Jesus said, *"At that time they will see the Son of Man coming in a cloud with power and great glory. When these things begin to take place, stand up and lift up your heads, **because your redemption is drawing near.**"*

Paul taught the same thing in his letters. To the Romans in 13:11 he said, *"And do this, understanding the present time. The hour has come for you to wake up from your slumber, because **our salvation is nearer now than when we first believed.**"* In Galatians 5:5 he said, *"But by faith we eagerly await through the Spirit the righteousness for which we hope."* And in Titus 2:11-14, *"For the grace of God that brings salvation has appeared to all men. It teaches us to say 'No' to ungodliness and worldly passions, and to live self-controlled, upright and godly lives in this present age, while we wait for the blessed hope—the glorious appearing of our great God and Savior, Jesus Christ, who gave himself for us to redeem us from all wickedness and to purify for himself a people that are his very own, eager to do what is good."*

The Apostle Peter was also guided by the Holy Spirit to teach the same expectation of the Lord's coming to signify the completion of the atonement and finish the work of salvation. In 1 Peter 1:3-7 he wrote, *"Praise be to the God and Father of our Lord Jesus Christ! In his great mercy he has given us new birth into a living hope through the resurrection of Jesus Christ from the dead, and into an inheritance that can never perish, spoil or fade—kept in heaven for you, who through faith are shielded by God's power **until the coming of the salvation that is ready to be revealed in the last time.** In this you greatly rejoice, though now for a little while you may have had to suffer grief in all kinds of trials. These have come so that your faith—of greater worth than gold, which perishes even though refined by fire—may be proved genuine and may result in praise, glory and honor when Jesus Christ is revealed."* Jesus was ready to be revealed

The Atonement Sacrifice

at the "last time," bringing to fruition the great mystery of God, completing the atonement ritual and God's plan of salvation.

This is why he left no doubt how everyone could tell he had returned. Jesus linked the destruction of Jerusalem, the temple, and the former Holy of Holies to that event. *"This is how you will know...when you see the abomination of desolation spoken of by the prophet Daniel, let the reader understand"* (Matt. 24). *"When you see Jerusalem surrounded by armies...this is the time of punishment in fulfillment of all that has been written...Stand up, lift up your heads,* **because your redemption is drawing near**" (Luke 21)! They both go on to say, *"This generation will certainly not pass away until all these things have happened."* Why the destruction of the temple as the final sign? It was the place of the atonement sacrifice. Once the real atonement was completed in heaven there was no need for the earthly temple. No more sacrifice for sin is required!

If the Lord did not "come again" as he promised and the Gospel writers predicted during that generation; if we are still awaiting his return, then the sacrifice of the High Priest was not accepted and our redemption is still not a reality. A careful study of Hebrews 9 makes this abundantly clear. In verse 8 the writer says that the sacrifice of the High Priest was the Spirit's way of *"...showing that the way into the Most Holy Place had not yet been disclosed* **as long as the first tabernacle was still standing**.*"* When one saw the old temple destroyed, one would KNOW that the sacrifice had been accepted and the way into the Most Holy Place was open for all! Christ was sacrificed once to take away the sins of all people; and was to appear a second time, not to bear sin, but to bring salvation to those who were waiting for him. This is the same "appearing of our Great God and Savior Jesus Christ" of whom Paul, Peter, James and all the other New Testament writers speak. We are NOT still waiting for salvation!

In chapter 10 the writer continues to parallel the old covenant with the new covenant of Jesus Christ. He explains how we

"...have confidence to enter the Most Holy Place by the blood of Jesus" (10:19). He encourages the Hebrew Christians to persevere through their trials and encourage each other more and more as they *"...see the Day approaching."* Isaiah, Joel and many other prophets had promised a "great and notable day of the Lord" would come to usher in the eternal kingdom and bring judgment on the nations. At the end of chapter 10 the encouragement is to hang on because *"...in just a little while* (literally soon, very soon) *he who is coming will come and not delay..."*

The writer here quotes from Habakkuk 2:3-4. The prophet's warnings were not only to the Jews of his day but also foreshadowed the coming events of Israel's "last days." We read in Acts 13:38-41, *"Therefore, my brothers, I want you to know that through Jesus the forgiveness of sins is proclaimed to you. Through him everyone who believes is justified from everything you could not be justified from by the Law of Moses. Take care that what the prophets have said does not happen to you: 'Look, you scoffers, wonder and perish, for I am going to do something in your days that you would never believe, even if someone told you.'"* Quoting from Habakkuk 1:5 Paul clearly confirmed that the prophecy saw its ultimate fulfillment in Jesus' death, resurrection and subsequent establishment of the church.

The author of Hebrews quotes from Habakkuk 2:3, *"For the revelation awaits an appointed time; it speaks of the end and will not prove false. Though it linger, wait for it; it will certainly come and will not delay."* What was coming and would not delay was the appearing of Jesus Christ to bring salvation to those who were waiting. There is no discrepancy between Acts and Hebrews. They were both discussing events that would occur in that generation. If we can simply believe what it says, the Bible interprets itself.

Hebrews chapter 12 concludes this concept with the explanation of God's "shaking the earth" to take away the physical kingdom so *"...what cannot be shaken may remain."* In verses 26-

29 it says, *"At that time his voice shook the earth, but now he has promised, 'Once more I will shake not only the earth but also the heavens.' The words 'once more' indicate the removing of what can be shaken—that is, created things—so that what cannot be shaken may remain. Therefore, since we are receiving a kingdom that cannot be shaken, let us be thankful, and so worship God acceptably with reverence and awe, for our God is a consuming fire."*

To understand what the Hebrew writer is saying we must first understand the prophesies from which he is quoting. In Isaiah 2 the prophet describes a coming time during the "last days" of Judah and Jerusalem when the Lord would establish his new eternal kingdom. At that time, in verse 19, he says, *"Men will flee to caves in the rocks and to holes in the ground from dread of the Lord and the splendor of his majesty, when he rises to shake the earth."*

So as not to leave anything to speculation, God set up a graphic demonstration to show what he meant by "shaking the earth." In 586 B.C. God brought the Babylonians to bring his judgment against Israel because of their disobedience just as he had warned them in Habakkuk chapter one. Jerusalem was overrun, the temple was desecrated, and they were carried off into captivity. Their world was indeed shaken. Then in Isaiah 13 the prophet tells what was going to happen to the Babylonian kingdom.

> *"See, the day of the Lord is coming —a cruel day, with wrath and fierce anger— to make the land desolate and destroy the sinners within it. The stars of heaven and their constellations will not show their light. The rising sun will be darkened and the moon will not give its light. I will punish the world for its evil, the wicked for their sins. I will put an end to the arrogance of the haughty and will humble the pride of the ruthless. I will make man scarcer than pure gold, more rare than the gold of Ophir. Therefore I will make the heavens tremble; and the earth will shake*

from its place at the wrath of the Lord Almighty, in the day of his burning anger" (Isaiah 13:9-13).

Notice in this description the prophetic language that was used to describe God's judgment against a nation. The heavens tremble; the earth shakes. The stars and constellations do not shine; the sun and moon are darkened. This was the description of his coming judgment on Babylon. The Medes came and overthrew their empire, and it was never rebuilt.

Then in Haggai 2:6-9 the Bible says,

"This is what the Lord Almighty says: 'In a little while I will once more shake the heavens and the earth, the sea and the dry land. I will shake all nations, and the desired of all nations will come, and I will fill this house with glory,' says the Lord Almighty. 'The silver is mine and the gold is mine,' declares the Lord Almighty. 'The glory of this present house will be greater than the glory of the former house,' says the Lord Almighty. 'And in this place I will grant peace,' declares the Lord Almighty."

Haggai lived after the Babylonian exile and was predicting the ultimate outcome of the kingdom of Israel. This "shaking of the earth" would result in a new house into which the desired of all nations would come. He also says the glory of the former house (temple in Jerusalem) would be replaced with a house far more glorious. To what else could the prophet be referring than the removal of the physical kingdom of Israel and the establishment of the eternal kingdom of God? That is also exactly what Isaiah had originally predicted.

Not surprisingly, Jesus quoted from some of the same verses and used the same imagery when telling his apostles about the coming destruction of Jerusalem in Matthew 24:29-30.

The Atonement Sacrifice

"Immediately after the distress of those days the sun will be darkened, and the moon will not give its light; the stars will fall from the sky, and the heavenly bodies will be shaken. At that time the sign of the Son of Man will appear in the sky, and all the nations of the earth will mourn. They will see the Son of Man coming on the clouds of the sky, with power and great glory."

Luke leaves no doubt when he explains this same discussion to his Gentile readers. Luke 21:20-28, *"When you see Jerusalem being surrounded by armies, you will know that its desolation is near... There will be signs in the sun, moon and stars. On the earth, nations will be in anguish and perplexity at the roaring and tossing of the sea. Men will faint from terror, apprehensive of what is coming on the world, for the heavenly bodies will be shaken. At that time they will see the Son of Man coming in a cloud with power and great glory. When these things begin to take place, stand up and lift up your heads, because your redemption is drawing near."* Given the prophetic history and background of this coming event, why would anyone be surprised to see the destruction of Jerusalem in the New Testament described in these very same terms? If it were not, how would we know it was the fulfillment of the prophetic Scriptures? One must have a lot of help to twist these Scriptures into a future coming of the Lord.

During the first century, between the first and second appearance of Jesus, they were receiving (present tense) a kingdom. God indeed "shook the earth," removing what could be shaken (the earthly kingdom of Israel) and leaving only that which cannot be shaken...the eternal kingdom, the church. We are not still awaiting the kingdom.

The writer of Hebrews, as well as the other New Testament writers, understood the consummation of the ages. Below is a simple chart showing the things that were changing during the consummation (fulfillment) of the ages. These things were all to happen during the "last days" of Judah and Jerusalem. When asked by his apostles when these things would happen and what would be the sign of his coming and the end of the age, Jesus' response was the destruction of Jerusalem and the temple would be the final sign that all was accomplished (Matthew 24). In 1 Corinthians 10:11 the Apostle Paul said the "fulfillment of the ages" had come upon the people of his generation.

Consummation of the Ages		
John the Baptist ←	Last Days	A.D. 70 →
Present Age		Age to Come
Kingdom of Israel		Kingdom of Heaven
Old Covenant		New Covenant
Law of Moses		Law of Grace
Levitical Priesthood		Priesthood of Believers
High Priest from Aaron		Jesus as High Priest
Physical City & temple		Heavenly City & Temple

CHAPTER 6

The Kingdom of Heaven

When the disciples of Jesus asked him to teach them to pray, one line in his model prayer was, *"Thy kingdom come."* For what were they supposed to pray? Did they understand what Jesus was telling them? How would they know if God answered this prayer? Is this still to be the prayer of Christians today? If one does not properly understand the Biblical concept of the "last days," it will be difficult indeed to determine the nature and establishment of the kingdom of heaven and whether or not God ever answered this prayer. This kingdom is the subject of the Scriptures from beginning to end because it is the dwelling place of all the redeemed. It is important that we understand what the Bible teaches about it.

When Adam and Eve sinned in the Garden of Eden, God told the Devil that day that someone who would come through the woman's offspring would crush his head. In Genesis 3:15 the Lord said, *"And I will put enmity between you and the woman, and between your offspring and hers; he will crush your head, and you will strike his heel."* Nobody at that time knew what, but something was coming.

As we follow the history of successive generations from Adam and Eve we see just how pervasive sin became. Finally God sent a worldwide flood that destroyed everyone except Noah and his family. Following that event man continued to sin, and it became abundantly clear Satan would not be crushed by destroying those who fell for his deceptive schemes. In Genesis 12:1-2, *"The Lord had said to Abram, 'Leave your country, your people and your father's household and go to the land I will show you. I will make you into a*

The Kingdom of Heaven

great nation and I will bless you; I will make your name great, and you will be a blessing.' " Abraham understood his descendants would become a nation. But somehow he also knew there was more to God's promise than just physical cities in a physical country. Hebrews 11:10 says, *"For he* (Abraham) *was looking forward to the city with foundations, whose architect and builder is God."* Abraham did not know exactly what, but something great was coming.

A few centuries passed, and Abraham's descendants ended up as slaves in Egypt. To the people living under the cruel taskmasters of the Pharaohs it must have felt like God had forgotten his promise to their ancestors. Yet all the while they were living in Egypt, God was blessing them with children, and their numbers were steadily growing. By the time they were finally led through the Red Sea to freedom, over a million people had become the independent nation of Israel. They had not yet come to their promised land, but they were the beginning of a great nation.

Exodus 19:3-6 tells us that when they reached Mt. Sinai the Lord called Moses up to meet with him and said, *"This is what you are to say to the house of Jacob and what you are to tell the people of Israel: 'You yourselves have seen what I did to Egypt, and how I carried you on eagles' wings and brought you to myself. Now if you obey me fully and keep my covenant, then out of all nations you will be my treasured possession. Although the whole earth is mine, you will be for me a kingdom of priests and a holy nation.' These are the words you are to speak to the Israelites."* For the first time we see this nation promised to Abraham was to become the kingdom of God. This was going to be no ordinary kingdom, but a kingdom of priests, a holy nation. Something special was coming.

In 1 Samuel 16 we read about the Lord sending the prophet Samuel to anoint David as king over Israel. David was the first king to reign over Israel by God's own choosing. (Saul was made king because of the people's demand to be like the other nations.

This was a sin against God, and none of his descendants succeeded him on the throne.) With David, the throne of Israel was now aligned with God's will, and it was established as an everlasting kingdom. David reigned seven years in Hebron, but after conquering the Jebusites who were living in Jerusalem, he made that the permanent capitol of the kingdom. 2 Samuel 5:9 tells us, *"David then took up residence in the fortress and called it the City of David."* He had the Ark of the Covenant brought to Jerusalem and placed in the tent tabernacle that was erected on what would be the future temple site.

With the tabernacle, the Holy of Holies, and the Ark of the Covenant now present, Jerusalem became not only the City of David, but also the City of God. It was in this tabernacle that God's presence dwelled. In spite of all the incredible things that had happened to David during his lifetime, he still knew there was more to come. In Psalm 16:9-10 he wrote, *"Therefore my heart is glad and my tongue rejoices; my body also will rest secure, because you will not abandon me to the grave, nor will you let your Holy One see decay."* The Apostle Peter said of David's words in Acts 2:29-31, *"Brothers, I can tell you confidently that the patriarch David died and was buried, and his tomb is here to this day. But he was a prophet and knew that God had promised him on oath that he would place one of his descendants on his throne. Seeing what was ahead, he spoke of the resurrection of the Christ, that he was not abandoned to the grave, nor did his body see decay."* David sat on his throne in the kingdom of God, but he knew something better was coming.

The prophet Nathan was sent to tell David about the throne and the kingdom in 2 Samuel 7:8-16.

> *"Now then, tell my servant David, 'This is what the Lord Almighty says: I took you from the pasture and from following the flock to be ruler over my people Israel. I have been with you wherever you have gone, and I have cut off all your enemies from before*

> *you. Now I will make your name great, like the names of the greatest men of the earth. And I will provide a place for my people Israel and will plant them so that they can have a home of their own and no longer be disturbed...The Lord declares to you that the Lord himself will establish a house for you: When your days are over and you rest with your fathers, I will raise up your offspring to succeed you, who will come from your own body, and I will establish his kingdom. He is the one who will build a house for my Name, and I will establish the throne of his kingdom forever...Your house and your kingdom will endure forever before me;* **your throne will be established forever.**'"

As we continue to follow the story, we know that David's son Solomon did build the temple for the Lord in Jerusalem. The temple was more than just a beautiful house of worship. It was built exactly as God had instructed Moses to build the tabernacle in the wilderness as a sanctuary for the Lord. This magnificent structure became the permanent tabernacle where God's presence would dwell in his kingdom on earth.

One can read about the building and dedication of the temple in 2 Chronicles chapters 1-9. It was this temple, not Solomon's palace, which became the symbol for the entire kingdom of Israel. Israel had indeed become the kingdom of God, and Jerusalem had become the place that bore his name, just as he had told the Jews in the wilderness when he gave them instructions about keeping the Passover Feast (Deuteronomy 16:5-8). With the building of the temple, Jerusalem was forever established as the City of God, and his kingdom would be everlasting, just as he had promised. Psalm 145:13, *"Your kingdom is an everlasting kingdom, and your dominion endures through all generations. The Lord is faithful to all his promises and loving toward all he has made."* But there was more coming…much more.

During the succeeding reign of the various kings in Jerusalem, the prophets were foretelling of a future king that would sit on David's throne in a New Jerusalem. Isaiah 9:6-7, *"For to us a child is born, to us a son is given, and the government will be on his shoulders. And he will be called Wonderful Counselor, Mighty God, Everlasting Father, Prince of Peace. Of the increase of his government and peace there will be no end. He will reign on David's throne and over his kingdom, establishing and upholding it with justice and righteousness from that time on and forever. The zeal of the Lord Almighty will accomplish this."*

Isaiah clearly identifies Jesus as the ultimate successor to David's throne and David's kingdom. David's throne and the kingdom of Israel had been set up by the God of heaven as a prototype of a future kingdom that would encompass the entire earth and endure forever. Daniel 2:44 says, *"In the time of those kings* (Roman Empire)*, the God of heaven will set up a kingdom that will never be destroyed, nor will it be left to another people. It will crush all those kingdoms and bring them to an end, but it will itself endure forever."*

However, following Solomon's reign the physical kingdom of Israel was divided and went through immense struggle. By the time Jesus arrived on the scene, it must have appeared to a lot of Jews that God had abandoned his promise about their kingdom and David's throne lasting forever. Not since the death of Zedekiah in 586 B.C. had there been a descendant of David on the throne in Jerusalem.

After hundreds of years of silence, God sent his angel to a young virgin in Judea to tell her she was going to have a baby. In Luke 1:32-34 the angel said, *"He will be great and will be called the Son of the Most High. The Lord God will give him the throne of his father David, and he will reign over the house of Jacob forever; his kingdom will never end."* God had not forgotten his promise. Everything was now in place for him to restore the kingdom and throne of David.

Almost thirty years following the announcement by the angel to Mary, John the Baptist began proclaiming, *"Repent, for the kingdom of heaven is near"* (Matthew 3:2). Jews of the first century were very familiar with the Old Testament prophesies concerning a coming Messiah who would sit on David's throne and *"...restore the fortunes of Judah and Jerusalem"* (Isaiah 9:6-7, Joel 3:1). John's preaching caused no small stir in Israel. Folks began to get excited about what was coming.

When Jesus was baptized by John, the Spirit of God descended on him and proclaimed him to be the Son of God. From that time on Jesus began to preach, *"Repent, for the kingdom of heaven is near"* (Matthew 4:17). Later Jesus sent his apostles out to preach the same message. In Matthew 10:5-7 we read where he sent them out with the following instructions: *"Do not go among the Gentiles or enter any town of the Samaritans. Go rather to the lost sheep of Israel. As you go, preach this message: 'The kingdom of heaven is near.'"* Why would they not go to the Gentiles with that message? It was to Abraham and his descendants that the promise was made. It was David's throne that was to be restored to last forever. The "good news" of the kingdom (Matthew 24:14) was first to be proclaimed to those to whom it had been promised. Just as Daniel had prophesied, *"He will confirm a covenant with many for one 'seven.' In the middle of the 'seven' he will put an end to sacrifice and offering. And on a wing of the temple he will set up an abomination that causes desolation, until the end that is decreed is poured out on him"* (Daniel 9:27). This promise was given specifically to the Jews. God was going to confirm his covenant with them first, after which the gospel would be preached to the Gentiles.

The kingdom of heaven was the subject of almost all of Jesus' parables and most of his other teachings. In Matthew 11:11-13 he said, *"I tell you the truth: Among those born of women there has not risen anyone greater than John the Baptist; yet he who is least in the kingdom of heaven is greater than he. From the days of John the Baptist until now, the kingdom of heaven has been forcefully advancing, and forceful men lay hold of it. For all the Prophets and the Law prophesied until John."* About what had all the Prophets and the Law before John prophesied? Obviously the coming kingdom of heaven, which was now near. In Luke 4:43 Jesus said the reason he was sent was to *"...preach the good news of the kingdom of God."*

As Jesus entered Jerusalem for the last time we read in Mark 11:9-10 that those who went ahead of him and those who followed shouted, *"Hosanna!" "Blessed is he who comes in the name of the Lord!" "Blessed is the coming kingdom of our father David!" "Hosanna in the highest!"* This coming kingdom of God would also be the restored kingdom of David. Jesus was born into the world through the tribe of Judah and thus was a descendant of David. He could rightfully claim the throne of David and fulfill all the promises of the Old Testament concerning the everlasting nature of the spiritual kingdom of Israel which would be the ultimate fulfillment of God's promise to Abraham.

Not only was the "good news" message of John, Jesus, and the apostles about a coming kingdom to fulfill the prophesies and "restore the fortunes of Judah and Jerusalem," but the time was "at hand." It was going to happen soon! In Matthew 16:28 Jesus said, *"I tell you the truth, some who are standing here will not taste death before they see the Son of Man coming in his kingdom."* Mark records this in Mark 9:1, *"I tell you the truth, some who are standing here will not taste death before they see the kingdom of God come with power."*

Jesus added a new twist to the story in Matthew 16:18-20. After asking his disciples who they thought he was, Peter replied that he was the Christ, the Son of God. Jesus said to him, *"And I*

The Kingdom of Heaven

tell you that you are Peter, and on this rock I will build **my church***, and the gates of Hades will not overcome it. I will give you the keys of* **the kingdom of heaven***; whatever you bind on earth will be bound in heaven, and whatever you loose on earth will be loosed in heaven."* Here Jesus identified the kingdom of heaven as the church which he was going to build. In his parable about the sheep and goats in Matthew 25:34 Jesus said the king would say, *"Come, you who are blessed by my Father; take your inheritance, the kingdom prepared for you since the creation of the world."* According to Jesus the inheritance of the righteous was this coming kingdom, the church, which had been prepared since creation.

The message was clear. The kingdom of God was coming, and some of them were even going to live to see it. The crowds grew, excitement was building, hope was at an all-time high. Then something seemed to go terribly wrong. Jesus was falsely accused, arrested, tried, sentenced, and crucified outside Jerusalem. All the hopes of his disciples, all their excitement, all their dreams died and were buried with him in that borrowed tomb.

Joseph must have had a heavy heart when he approached Pilate for Jesus' body. Mark 15:43 tells us, *"Joseph of Arimathea, a prominent member of the Council,* **who was himself waiting for the kingdom of God***, went boldly to Pilate and asked for Jesus' body."* He had been waiting for the kingdom and fully believed this was the time. Now he was asking for the body of the person he had thought was the One.

The apostles and other disciples scattered. Peter, James and John went back to fishing. Perhaps the utter disappointment was best expressed by the ones going home to Emmaus. *"We had hoped that he was the one who was going to redeem Israel."* (Luke 24:21). One can feel the sadness in those words. They were living examples of one of King Solomon's proverbs, *"Hope deferred makes the heart sick"* (Proverbs 13:12).

But as soon as those heavy words were spoken, Jesus said to them, *"How foolish you are, and how slow of heart to believe all that the prophets have spoken! Did not the Christ have to suffer these things and then enter his glory? And beginning with Moses and all the Prophets, he explained to them what was said in all the Scriptures concerning himself"* (Luke 24:25-27). As soon as they realized he had really come back from the grave, they hurried back to Jerusalem to tell the other disciples. By this time the news was spreading like wild fire. HE IS ALIVE!

Hope was reborn. The story was far from over. Something wonderful was still coming. Jesus had tried to explain all this to them prior to his death, but they just could not believe it. After all, David died and was still dead. So were all his successors. Why would the next king to sit on his throne be any different?

Jesus, standing trial before Pilate, in John 18:36-37, explained the true nature of his kingdom. *"My kingdom is not of this world. If it were, my servants would fight to prevent my arrest by the Jews. But now my kingdom is from another place." "You are a king, then!" said Pilate. Jesus answered, "You are right in saying I am a king. In fact, for this reason I was born, and for this I came into the world..."* Jesus had come to be the king of the Jews, but it was the nature of his kingdom people did not understand. *"Once, having been asked by the Pharisees when the kingdom of God would come, Jesus replied, The kingdom of God does not come with your careful observation, nor will people say, 'Here it is,' or 'There it is,' because the kingdom of God is within you"* (Luke 17:20-21). Jesus' kingdom was going to be a spiritual kingdom, not a physical one. The ultimate fulfillment of God's promise to the patriarchs was this new spiritual kingdom. The real tragedy of sin is spiritual death; the victory we have through Jesus Christ is spiritual life. The physical was only a prototype of the coming spiritual. They didn't get it...neither do many Christians today.

The Kingdom of Heaven

With the resurrection of Jesus came a renewed excitement and hope for the future. Now would the kingdom be restored? That was what the apostles wanted to know. We read in Acts 1:1-8:

"In my former book, Theophilus, I wrote about all that Jesus began to do and to teach until the day he was taken up to heaven, after giving instructions through the Holy Spirit to the apostles he had chosen. After his suffering, he showed himself to these men and gave many convincing proofs that he was alive. He appeared to them over a period of forty days and spoke about the kingdom of God. On one occasion, while he was eating with them, he gave them this command: 'Do not leave Jerusalem, but wait for the gift my Father promised, which you have heard me speak about. For John baptized with water, but in a few days you will be baptized with the Holy Spirit.'

So when they met together, they asked him, **'Lord, are you at this time going to restore the kingdom to Israel?'** *He said to them: 'It is not for you to know the times or dates the Father has set by his own authority. But you will receive power when the Holy Spirit comes on you; and you will be my witnesses in Jerusalem, and in all Judea and Samaria, and to the ends of the earth.' "*

His resurrection convinced his disciples he was the one to restore the kingdom. However, they still did not understand when or how, although he had explained this to them prior to his death. Most Jews believed the Messiah would come, raise an army, defeat the Romans, set up an earthly kingdom and physically reign on David's throne. Many Jews tragically missed their own Messiah because they could not understand and accept the spiritual nature of his kingdom. They wanted a physical kingdom, a physical king, so they refused to believe Jesus. It is even more amazing that a majority of Christians today have believed the same false doctrine concerning the coming king and his kingdom. They have been told Jesus will physically return to the earth to establish his kingdom and reign on David's physical throne in a rebuilt city of Jerusalem for a thousand years. If that is the case, where does that leave Christians today? If the church and the kingdom are one and the same, as Jesus taught, how is this possible? Has the church not yet been established? The theology of this teaching is completely foreign to Scripture.

Jesus taught otherwise during his earthly ministry. He plainly said his kingdom was *"not of this world"* and it *"would not come visibly."* He also taught when it would come. In his instructions to the apostles recorded in Matthew 24-25, Mark 13, and Luke 21, he told them his kingdom would come the same time the old physical one was removed from the earth. That is how they would know when it was completed. Luke 21:20 Jesus said, *"When you see Jerusalem being surrounded by armies, you will know that its desolation is near."* A few verses later in that same discussion he said, *"Even so, when you see these things happening, you know that **the kingdom of God is near**. I tell you the truth, this generation will certainly not pass away until all these things have happened"* (Luke 21:31-32).

In his parable of the talents Jesus continued teaching the same time frame for the coming of the kingdom. Matthew's account of this parable begins, *"Again, it will be like a man going on a journey, who called his servants and entrusted his property to them..."* (Matthew 25:14). Keeping Matthew in its context, we see Jesus was still speaking of the day of the Lord when the temple and its buildings would be destroyed. He has not changed the subject from chapter 24.

Luke 19:11-13 clearly links this parable with the coming kingdom. *"While they were listening to this, he went on to tell them a parable, because he was near Jerusalem and the people thought that the kingdom of God was going to appear at once. He said: A man of noble birth went to a distant country to have himself appointed king and then to return. So he called ten of his servants and gave them ten minas. Put this money to work, he said, until I come back."*

What were the people expecting? Jesus was going to Jerusalem, and they thought the kingdom of God was going to come immediately when he got there. The story of the parable is about *"...a man of noble birth who was going away to have himself appointed king and then return."* Jesus was the noble man who was going to become the King of Kings. We know the kingdom had not come prior to his death, and we know it had still not come following his resurrection. If it had, his disciples would not have asked in Acts 1 when it was coming. In the parable Jesus said when the man of noble birth first has to go away to be anointed king, then he would return. The instruction to his disciples was for them to be good stewards until he returned as king. When did that happen? When did the kingdom come?

As we continue through the Acts of the Apostles and the letters in the New Testament we find the Holy Spirit guided the first century disciples and writers to continue teaching about the coming kingdom. In 2 Timothy 4:1 the Apostle Paul tells young Timothy, *"In the presence of God and of Christ Jesus, who will judge the living and the dead, and **in view of his appearing and his kingdom**, I give you this charge: Preach the word…"* Evidently the appearing of Jesus and his kingdom were still in Paul's and Timothy's future. They were also inextricably linked together.

The writer of Hebrews discussed in great length the change from the Old Law to the New Covenant in Christ, from the physical kingdom of the Jews to the spiritual kingdom of Jesus. He also clearly recognized this change was still in progress and would be completed when the Lord returned **during their lifetime**. In chapter 10:36-37 he said, *"You need to persevere so that* *when you have done the will of God, you will receive what he has promised. For in just a very little while, he who is coming will come and will not delay."* Then in chapter 12:26-29, he spoke of the removal of the old and the coming of the new when he said, *"At that time* (giving of the Old Law on Mt. Sinai) *his voice shook the earth, but now he has promised, 'Once more I will shake not only the earth but also the heavens.' The words 'once more' indicate the removing of what can be shaken—that is, created things—so that what cannot be shaken may remain. Therefore,* **since we are receiving a kingdom** *that cannot be shaken, let us be thankful, and so worship God acceptably with reverence and awe, for our God is a consuming fire."*

The giving of the old Law of Moses on Mt. Sinai led to the eventual building of the temple in Jerusalem where God's presence dwelled during the days of the physical nation of Israel. All these physical (created) things could be "shaken" or removed from the earth. The physical nation had been shaken in the past and even the sacred furnishings of that physical temple had been carried off into foreign countries. God was replacing the physical kingdom with a spiritual one that could not be shaken. According to the author of Hebrews, that spiritual kingdom was still coming at the time of his writing and would be complete when Jesus returned. He said we *are receiving* (not *have received*) a kingdom.

So when did the kingdom come, or is it still coming? If the parable is true and Jesus has not yet been crowned king, the kingdom cannot be a reality. You cannot have a kingdom without a king. Since the kingdom and the church are one and the same, that would mean the church has not yet been established. Another possibility is that the church was established on the Day of Pentecost (Acts 2) and since the church is also the kingdom, that is when the kingdom came. This explanation cannot be correct since the passages in Timothy and Hebrews, written three decades after Pentecost, clearly state that the kingdom, as well as Jesus' appearing, was still to occur in the future.

If the coming of Jesus is to be at the "end of time," that would mean neither the kingdom nor the church will ever exist in this world. The only possibility that makes any sense is to simply believe what Jesus said. He said he was going away to become king, and he would return in his kingdom. He also taught the new spiritual kingdom will replace the old physical one and fulfill all the prophesies of Old Testament Scripture. Further, he said when the armies came and destroyed the temple in Jerusalem, that would be the sign that all these things had been completed. To make sure we didn't miss it, he said, *"This generation will not pass away until all these things have happened."*

Jesus ascended to the Father. He went away to be anointed king. During the time he was away he sent the Holy Spirit to reveal to the apostles (and others) the New Covenant of the spiritual kingdom. Once that revelation was complete, he returned, destroyed the physical temple and Jerusalem (what could be shaken), thus fulfilling the final prophesies concerning the consummation of the ages. The kingdom of God and David's throne were now fully established in the Heavens where they can never again be shaken.

The Apostle John was privileged to witness the events of that great "day of the Lord" when the physical kingdom of Israel (the prototype) became the kingdom of God (the reality). Revelation 11:15 says, *"The seventh angel sounded his trumpet, and there were loud voices in heaven, which said: 'The kingdom of the world has become the kingdom of our Lord and of his Christ, and he will reign for ever and ever.' "* The book of Revelation is about this consummation of God's plan to complete his eternal plan for redemption and establish the eternal kingdom. It is the Revelation of Jesus Christ, not the revelation of some imagined end of the world.

And what about God's promise to the devil in Genesis? Revelation 12:10, *"Then I heard a loud voice in heaven say: 'Now have come the salvation and the power and the kingdom of our God, and the authority of his Christ. For the accuser of our brothers, who accuses them before our God day and night, has been hurled down.'"* The Apostle Paul had written about this just a few years earlier in Romans 16:20. *"The God of peace will soon crush Satan under your feet."* In 1 John 3:8 Jesus said, *"He who does what is sinful is of the devil, because the devil has been sinning from the beginning. The reason the Son of God appeared was to destroy the devil's work."*

Remember, God had told Satan one of the woman's descendants would crush his head. Jesus did.

Remember, God had promised Abraham that his "seed" would bless the whole world. Jesus did.

Remember, God had promised David one of his descendants would reign on his throne forever. Jesus does.

Remember, God promised the kingdom of Israel would become an eternal kingdom that would never end, and Jesus said this promised kingdom of heaven was his church.

His kingdom came.

The prayer was answered.

JESUS REIGNS!

CHAPTER 7

What Did Jesus Really Say?

When one considers how much time Jesus spent teaching about the coming destruction of Jerusalem and its temple, and the significance of this event related to the coming spiritual kingdom, it seems rather amazing that most Christians today have never studied the subject and consider it virtually irrelevant to their lives. This has given rise to a seemingly endless number of unchallenged prophecies based on his words. While the theories may seem plausible and the Bible references they use may seem to fit their stories, are they really what Jesus was teaching?

Jesus was the One who said he was coming again. He explained what signs to look for as the time approached. It seems fitting to put all the three accounts of Jesus' own explanation side by side and simply see what he said. As much as possible, we should strive to put aside our preconceived ideas, and ask one simple question.

What did Jesus really say?

We will spend this chapter looking specifically at what Jesus taught would happen and when he said all these things would occur. Three of the Gospel writers included Jesus' teachings on the subject in their narratives. Matthew and Mark are written from the Jewish perspective. Luke's account is written to a Gentile in language more easily understood by someone not steeped in Jewish tradition. All three accounts tell of the same events and the same time of fulfillment. Since they are all inspired by the Holy Spirit, they are in total agreement on the truth. Most of us share Luke's Gentile heritage; therefore, his account is particularly helpful to us in understanding some of the Old Testament prophecies being fulfilled by these events.

What Did Jesus Really Say?

We will begin by comparing the three parallel accounts. The charts in this section list some of the major points Jesus made and how the same message is conveyed to different readers so all can understand. Each chart contains questions or statements that are parallel; that is, they are expressing the exact same part of Jesus' message in their own individual linguistic style as divinely guided by the Holy Spirit. In addition to comparing the three accounts of the actual text we will also examine a few other Scriptural passages which refer to this same conversation.

Matthew 24	Mark 13	Luke 21
¹ Jesus left the temple and was walking away when his disciples came up to him to call his attention to its buildings.	*¹ As he was leaving the temple, one of his disciples said to him, "Look, Teacher! What massive stones! What magnificent buildings!"*	*⁵ Some of his disciples were remarking about how the temple was adorned with beautiful stones and with gifts dedicated to God.*

The Bible begins the narrative by unmistakably identifying the subject of the conversation. Jesus and his disciples were leaving the temple area and the disciples were commenting on the marvelous structures. In the above passage we see how each writer introduced the subject, calling attention to the temple buildings and their construction.

Matthew 24	Mark 13	Luke 21
² "I tell you the truth, not one stone here will be left on another; every one will be thrown down."	*² "Not one stone here will be left on another; every one will be thrown down."*	*⁶ "As for what you see here, the time will come when not one stone will be left on another; every one of them will be thrown down."*

Jesus is Coming Soon?

Jesus immediately said something that shocked them. These beautiful buildings with their massive stones would be utterly destroyed! *"Not one stone will be left on another."* The temple, and all its surrounding buildings, would be completely gone.

Matthew 24	Mark 13	Luke 21
³As Jesus was sitting on the Mount of Olives, the disciples came to him privately. "Tell us," they said, "when will this happen, and what will be the sign of your coming and of the end of the age?"	*³As Jesus was sitting on the Mount of Olives opposite the temple, Peter, James, John and Andrew asked him privately, ⁴"Tell us, when will these things happen? And what will be the sign that they are all about to be fulfilled?"*	*⁷"Teacher," they asked, "when will these things happen? And what will be the sign that they are about to take place?"*

This led to two obvious questions from the disciples. WHEN WILL THIS HAPPEN? HOW WILL WE KNOW? Some teachers, in an effort to support their own world view, take the account in Matthew, ignoring Mark and Luke, and say there were actually multiple questions about different events, then proceed to divide Matthew 24 into sections with Jesus answering these very different questions and discussing entirely different historical periods of time. How many questions did the disciples ask and how many did Jesus answer? Were the questions about one event, or multiple events? The answer is clear when we compare the three accounts.

Luke says, *"When will these things* (destruction of temple buildings) *happen? And what will be the sign that they* (same things) *are all* (not some) *about to be fulfilled?"* Mark says about the same in his account; *"When will these things happen? And what will be the sign that they are about to take place?"* There is only one subject being discussed, the destruction of the temple buildings, and only one subject of the disciples' questions. They wanted to know when this would happen and what would be the signs that it was about to take place. Matthew was not wrong in his recording of the questions when he referred to the Lord's coming and the end of the age. Writing from his Jewish perspective and understanding Old Testament prophecies, he knew the destruction of Jerusalem and its temple would be at the "coming of the Son of Man" to establish the eternal kingdom (Daniel 7:13-14) and be at the "end of the age (world-KJV)" (Daniel 7). The writer of Hebrews confirms the time in which they were living as this "age-ending" time. Hebrews 9:26 says, *"But now he (Christ) has appeared once for all* **at the end of the ages** *to do away with sin by the sacrifice of himself."* Matthew did not record different questions, nor did he record questions about different subjects or time periods. The three gospel accounts are in perfect agreement. They do, however, shed light on the subject from differing perspectives. The subject is still the temple buildings and the questions are about when they will be destroyed and the signs that will precede this great age-changing event.

Matthew 24	Mark 13	Luke 21
₄*Jesus answered: "Watch out that no one deceives you. ₅For many will come in my name, claiming, 'I am the Christ,' and will deceive many.*	₅*Jesus said to them: "Watch out that no one deceives you. ₆Many will come in my name, claiming, 'I am he,' and will deceive many*	₈*He replied: "Watch out that you are not deceived. For many will come in my name, claiming, 'I am he,' and, 'The time is near.' Do not follow them*

Jesus is Coming Soon?

Jesus then began to answer their questions, and he first cautioned them to watch out for false teachers (false or "anti" christs) who would try to deceive people about what was going to take place. It was critical in the teaching of Jesus for people to properly understand these events. It is just as critical today if we are to comprehend the age-changing nature of his sacrifice on the cross which made it possible for the old temple, with its animal sacrifices, to finally be destroyed. This is fundamental to understanding our atonement and the eternal kingdom (church) which he was about to bring to fruition.

It is interesting to note how many modern religious prophets are still predicting the coming of the "antichrist" to usher in the return of Jesus and the establishment of his sovereign reign. The Apostle John was the only Bible author who used the word "antichrist" (antichristos). The term appears four times in his writings and he makes it very clear that he understood their coming as one of the signs Jesus said to watch for, and further identified that time in which he was living as "the last hour." In 1 John 2:18-22 he said, *"Dear children, this is the last hour; and as you have heard that the antichrist is coming, even now many antichrists have come. This is how we know it is the last hour."* Again in 1 John 4:3, *"But every spirit that does not acknowledge Jesus is not from God. This is the spirit of the antichrist, which you have heard is coming and **even now is already in the world.**"* John said the spirit of the antichrist, which they had been told was coming, was already in the world, which is how he knew it was the last hour. The only other conversation recorded in the Bible about false or "antichrists" was that of Jesus in his description of signs that would precede the destruction of Jerusalem and its temple buildings. There is not one Scripture that mentions any other coming of some "antichrist." If we are to believe the Bible, the antichrist came, just as Jesus and John said, prior to the destruction of the temple. There is no mysterious "antichrist" in our future.

Matthew 24	Mark 13	Luke 21
₆You will hear of wars and rumors of wars, but see to it that you are not alarmed. Such things must happen, but the end is still to come. ₇Nation will rise against nation, and kingdom against kingdom. There will be famines and earthquakes in various places. ₈All these are the beginning of birth pains.	₇When you hear of wars and rumors of wars, do not be alarmed. Such things must happen, but the end is still to come. ₈Nation will rise against nation, and kingdom against kingdom. There will be earthquakes in various places, and famines. These are the beginning of birth pains.	₉When you hear of wars and revolutions, do not be frightened. These things must happen first, but the end will not come right away." ₁₀"Nation will rise against nation, and kingdom against kingdom. ₁₁There will be great earthquakes, famines and pestilences in various places, and fearful events and great signs from heaven.

Jesus then told the disciples there would be "wars and rumors of wars," but they should not be too alarmed because the end will not come right away. Why the warning about wars? Practically every decade of human history has had its share of wars and rumors of war. The first century was no exception, but Jesus was talking about a particular war. There would be only one war in all of human history that would utterly destroy the temple and its buildings, as well as the entire Jewish world, to complete extinction. That they would be destroyed in a seemingly "human" war was God's plan, but not just any war and not just any time. It would happen in God's time and in a "God-directed" war. That's why he gave them many other signs and told them the end would not come right away. Keeping within the context of the subject,

Jesus is Coming Soon?

Jesus was talking about the end of the temple and the Jewish world…not the end of the physical universe. The end of the temple, its complete and total annihilation, came at the hands of the Romans in A.D. 70. Just as Jesus had predicted, John was the only apostle who "remained alive" until these things happened.

Matthew 24	Mark 13	Luke 21
₉"Then you will be handed over to be persecuted and put to death, and you will be hated by all nations because of me.	₉"You must be on your guard. You will be handed over to the local councils and flogged in the synagogues. On account of me you will stand before governors and kings as witnesses to them.	₁₂"But before all this, they will lay hands on you and persecute you. They will deliver you to synagogues and prisons, and you will be brought before kings and governors, and all on account of my name.

The apostles would be persecuted and tortured before this time would come. Jesus was telling them of things that would signify his coming. If this time is still to come, the first century persecution of the apostles would have had little or no meaning. He has not changed the subject.

Matthew 24	Mark 13	Luke 21
₁₄And this gospel of the kingdom will be preached in the whole world as a testimony to all nations, and then the end will come.	₁₀And the gospel must first be preached to all nations.	₁₃This will result in your being witnesses to them.

Prior to the destruction of the Jewish temple, the Gospel would be preached among all nations of that day. The apostles were commissioned by Jesus Himself to *"...go into all the world and preach the gospel to every nation."* That great commission was, and is, the mission of the church in every generation, but it had "age-changing" implications in the first century and specifically applied to the Jewish world. Before God would take away the temple and its worship under the Law of Moses, he would first announce the New Covenant to his chosen people. As we learn from Daniel's prophecy, he would confirm a covenant with his people for one "seven." Once they had been informed of the "new and better covenant" in Jesus Christ, the old temple had no further use. As Matthew's account says, *"Then the end will come."* He was still speaking of the end of the temple and surrounding buildings. This "sign" of the end of the age was fulfilled in that generation. Representatives of every nation heard the very first gospel sermon. Acts 2:5 describes the crowd gathered. *"Now there were staying in Jerusalem God-fearing Jews from every nation under heaven."* In Romans 1:8 Paul said the faith of the Roman Christians was being reported *"all over the world."* And this same apostle said in Colossians 1:23, *"This is the gospel that you heard and that has been proclaimed to every creature under heaven, and of which I, Paul, have become a servant."* If only every generation of Christians could make the same claim.

Jesus then explained how this event would fulfill the prophecy of Daniel. Matthew and Mark, being Jewish and understanding the significance of that prophetic event, give us the prophecy-fulfilling account. So we Gentiles would understand, Luke put it in "plain Greek" and simply said, when you see Jerusalem being surrounded by armies...RUN! All three described the same event, the coming destruction of Jerusalem and its temple. Thanks to Luke we know for sure what time frame Daniel was talking about in his prophecy.

Matthew 24	Mark 13	Luke 21
$_{15}$So when you see standing in the holy place 'the abomination that causes desolation, spoken of through the prophet Daniel—let the reader understand—$_{16}$then let those who are in Judea flee to the mountains.	$_{14}$When you see 'the abomination that causes desolation' standing where it does not belong—let the reader understand—then let those who are in Judea flee to the mountains.	$_{20}$When you see Jerusalem being surrounded by armies, you will know that its desolation is near. $_{21}$Then let those who are in Judea flee to the mountains, let those in the city get out, and let those in the country not enter the city.

One might wonder, if the city was surrounded by Roman armies, how anyone could escape. The answer to that dilemma comes from the historical records of the Roman Empire. In A.D. 66 there was a fairly successful revolt against the Roman armies in Jerusalem. In A.D. 67 the Emperor Nero sent his general Vespasian to squash the uprising and restore Rome's credibility and dominance as the world power. He completely surrounded the city of Jerusalem and was preparing for a final assault. Before he could implement his plan, news of Nero's death came. Vespasian withdrew his troops and went back to Rome where, after some months of upheaval in the empire, in December A.D. 69 he became the Emperor. In A.D. 70 Vespasian sent his son Titus to finish the job he had started in Judea. Anyone who listened to Jesus and was watching for the signs would have had ample opportunity to flee the city between sieges. God works in mysterious ways!

Matthew 24	Mark 13	Luke 21
	₂₂For this is the time of punishment in fulfillment of all that has been written.	₂₂For this is the time of punishment in fulfillment of all that has been written.

Matthew continually related his writing to the fulfillment of prophecy knowing his Jewish readers would readily recognize and understand what he was talking about. The Holy Spirit, not leaving anything to speculation, inspired both Mark and Luke to include Jesus' statement that this would be in fulfillment of all that had been written. That is a very important point, especially to non-Jewish folks who may not have the grasp of Old Testament prophecies Matthew's audience had. It also leads one to ask, if that event was the fulfillment of "all that has been written," where is the basis for future "age-ending" prophecies? The Bible here clearly says the events that transpired up to and including the destruction of the temple were all that had been prophesied about the "coming of the Lord" and the "end of the ages."

Jesus is Coming Soon?

Matthew 24	Mark 13	Luke 21
₁₉How dreadful it will be in those days for pregnant women and nursing mothers! ₂₀Pray that your flight will not take place in winter or on the Sabbath. ₂₁For then there will be great distress, unequaled from the beginning of the world until now—and never to be equaled again. ₂₂If those days had not been cut short, no one would survive, but for the sake of the elect those days will be shortened.	₁₇How dreadful it will be in those days for pregnant women and nursing mothers! ₁₈Pray that this will not take place in winter, ₁₉because those will be days of distress unequaled from the beginning, when God created the world, until now—and never to be equaled again. ₂₀If the Lord had not cut short those days, no one would survive. But for the sake of the elect, whom he has chosen, he has shortened them.	₂₃How dreadful it will be in those days for pregnant women and nursing mothers! There will be great distress in the land and wrath against this people. ₂₄They will fall by the sword and will be taken as prisoners to all the nations. Jerusalem will be trampled on by the Gentiles until the times of the Gentiles are fulfilled.

 Next Jesus talked about the intense persecution that would accompany those times. He said it would be a time of distress *"...unequaled from the beginning, when God created the world, until now...and never to be equaled again."* This was exactly what Daniel prophesied would happen in Daniel 12:1, *"At that time Michael, the great prince who protects your people, will arise. There will be a time of distress such as has not happened from the beginning of nations until then. But at that time your people—everyone whose name is found written in the book—will be delivered."* If what happened leading up to and during the destruction of Jerusalem and its temple buildings was a time of distress "never to be equaled again," how can anyone today predict a more terrible time still coming in our future?

Matthew 24	Mark 13	Luke 21
29*Immediately after the distress of those days the sun will be darkened, and the moon will not give its light; the stars will fall from the sky, and the heavenly bodies will be shaken.'*	24*But in those days, following that distress, the sun will be darkened, and the moon will not give its light;* 25*the stars will fall from the sky, and the heavenly bodies will be shaken.*	25*There will be signs in the sun, moon and stars. On the earth, nations will be in anguish and perplexity at the roaring and tossing of the sea.* 26*Men will faint from terror, apprehensive of what is coming on the world, for the heavenly bodies will be shaken.*

All three writers recorded Jesus as saying *"the heavenly bodies will be shaken."* What is the significance of this phrase? As we have already noted, this is but one more example of New Testament events fulfilling Old Testament prophecy. In Isaiah 2, speaking of all the events that would unfold when God established his eternal kingdom, the church, verse 19 says, *"Men will flee to caves in the rocks and to holes in the ground from dread of the Lord and the splendor of his majesty, when he rises to shake the earth."* Again in

Haggai 2:6-9, speaking of the future fulfillment of Israel's promises and how that future spiritual temple will far surpass the former physical one, *"This is what the Lord Almighty says: 'In a little while I will once more shake the heavens and the earth, the sea and the dry land. I will shake all nations, and the desired of all nations will come, and I will fill this house with glory,' says the Lord Almighty. 'The silver is mine and the gold is mine,' declares the Lord Almighty. 'The glory of this present house will be greater than the glory of the former house,' says the Lord Almighty. 'And in this place I will grant peace,' declares the Lord Almighty."* We see clearly the fulfillment of these prophecies in Hebrews where in chapter twelve he so vividly compared the receiving of the Old Covenant of Moses with receiving the New Covenant in Christ and in verses 26-29 said, *"At that time his voice shook the earth, but now he has promised, 'Once more I will shake not only the earth but also the heavens.' The words 'once more' indicate the removing of what can be shaken—that is, created things—so that what cannot be shaken may remain. Therefore, since we are receiving a kingdom that cannot be shaken, let us be thankful, and so worship God acceptably with reverence and awe, for our "God is a consuming fire."*

The "shaking of the earth" was a term applied to the removal of the old physical kingdom of Israel and its earthly temple to be replaced with the new spiritual kingdom, the church, and the Heavenly temple in which all the redeemed have access to the Holy of Holies. A large portion of the book of Hebrews deals with the significance of this "age-changing" event when the physical temple was being replaced with the spiritual one. In chapter 9:9 the writer put particular emphasis on the destruction of the physical one when he said, *"The Holy Spirit was showing by this that the way into the Most Holy Place had not yet been disclosed as long as the first tabernacle was still standing."* You may be thinking, "I thought the Holy of Holies was opened when Jesus died on the cross and the veil was symbolically torn." Jesus' death on that cross was the sacrifice that opened the way, but not until he took his blood into the very presence of God and offered it for our sins were we actually granted forgiveness. This is an exact parallel with the annual sacrifice of the High Priest under the Old Covenant which was covered in detail in our discussion of the Hebrew letter.

In case anyone still wonders when and where all this was to happen, Luke said *"Jerusalem will be trampled on..."* Neither the context nor the subject has changed. Jesus was still answering the same two questions: when will these buildings be destroyed, and what will be the signs this event is about to happen?

If we believe Daniel, we must also believe that the archangel Michael was present and guiding the events as they unfolded and every righteous person who had ever lived was finally cleansed by the blood of Jesus and delivered from death. And it gets even more exciting...read on!

Matthew 24	Mark 13	Luke 21
$_{30}$*They will see the Son of Man coming on the clouds of the sky, with power and great glory. $_{31}$And he will send his angels with a loud trumpet call, and they will gather his elect from the four winds, from one end of the heavens to the other.*	$_{26}$*At that time men will see the Son of Man coming in clouds with great power and glory. $_{27}$And he will send his angels and gather his elect from the four winds, from the ends of the earth to the ends of the heavens.*	$_{27}$*At that time they will see the Son of Man coming in a cloud with power and great glory. $_{28}$When these things begin to take place, stand up and lift up your heads, because your redemption is drawing near."*

Jesus would come in the clouds of the sky with power and great glory! How was this possible? Did he physically return to earth when the temple was destroyed? Let us examine the Scriptures. When Moses received the Old Covenant on Mt. Sinai the presence of God was in the form of a cloud. Exodus 24:15-16, *"When Moses went up on the mountain, the cloud covered it, and the glory of the Lord settled on Mount Sinai. For six days the cloud covered the mountain, and on the seventh day the Lord called to Moses from within the cloud."* Moses did not physically see God…he, and the Israelites, saw the cloud.

When the tabernacle was built and God descended to fill the Tent of Meeting, the Bible says in Exodus 40:34-35, *"Then the cloud covered the Tent of Meeting, and the glory of the Lord filled the tabernacle. Moses could not enter the Tent of Meeting because the cloud had settled upon it, and the glory of the Lord filled the tabernacle."* The children of Israel did not physically see God…they saw him in a cloud.

In Acts 1:9-11 the apostles watched as Jesus was taken up and hidden from their sight…in a cloud. *"After he said this, he was taken up before their very eyes, and a cloud hid him from their sight. They were looking intently up into the sky as he was going, when suddenly two men dressed in white stood beside them. 'Men of Galilee,' they said, 'why do you stand here looking into the sky? This same Jesus, who has been taken from you into heaven, will come back in the same way you have seen him go into heaven.'"* How had they seen him go? In a cloud. What was the purpose of the cloud? To hide him from their sight. How did he say he would return? In a cloud. Does that imply he could be physically seen? Just the opposite. Jesus said, *"My kingdom does not come visibly"* (Luke 17:20).

Those who teach a future coming of Jesus base much of their logic on this passage in Acts. They reason that since he was physically seen ascending and the angels said he would come back in the same manner, his return must also be physical. This point is usually made in connection with what John said in Revelation 1:7,

"Look, he is coming with the clouds, and every eye will see him, even those who pierced him; and all the peoples of the earth will mourn because of him. So shall it be! Amen."

One must first question the inconsistency of connecting these two passages to prove a physical return of Jesus. Applied in this way the two reasons are mutually exclusive. Jesus' literal ascension was witnessed by only a handful of people…not every person in the world. If he is going to return in exactly the same manner as he left, only a handful will see his return. In addition, if he is going to literally return to Jerusalem with the same body in which he left, only a few people could see him, not "every eye." How could someone in the Americas possibly see a physical person in Jerusalem? At some point everyone who espouses a view of the second coming must admit it will be vastly different from his ascension. Scripture says at the time of Jesus' ascension the clouds **concealed him from view.** This is exactly why the angels said he will come again "in like manner," and Jesus personally said he would come "in the clouds," concealed from view.

The "coming of the Lord" was not a foreign concept to the disciples to whom Jesus was speaking. The phrase was used repeatedly in Old Testament Scripture referring to God's coming in judgment on nations and in prophecies about this very time Jesus was describing and is often described as his "coming in the clouds." In Isaiah 19:1, *"An oracle concerning Egypt: See, the Lord rides on a swift cloud and is coming to Egypt. The idols of Egypt tremble before him, and the hearts of the Egyptians melt within them."* How was the Lord going to "come on a cloud" to Egypt? He came in exactly the same way he came to destroy the temple, in the form of an invading army.

Again In Isaiah 26:21, *"See, the Lord is coming out of his dwelling to punish the people of the earth for their sins."* And in Isaiah 66:6, *"Hear that uproar from the city, hear that noise from the temple! It is the sound of the Lord repaying his enemies all they deserve."* In verse 15 of the same chapter he says, *"See, the Lord is coming with fire, and his chariots are like a whirlwind; he will bring down his anger with fury, and his rebuke with flames of fire."* And in Micah 1:3, *"Look! The Lord is coming from his dwelling place; he comes down and treads the high places of the earth."*

The prophecy of the Lord's coming to destroy Jerusalem was described in Daniel 7:13, *"In my vision at night I looked, and there before me was one like a son of man, coming with the clouds of heaven. He approached the Ancient of Days and was led into his presence."*

That Jesus would use the same language to describe the age-changing events that were about to take place did not surprise his disciples, nor should it confuse any student of the Bible today. Not one example of the Lord coming in the clouds involved a physical sighting of the Almighty. When Jesus lived on earth, he had a physical body people could see and touch. Following his death, burial, resurrection, and ascension he resumed his role as God. He is Spirit, and human eyes cannot see spiritual beings. Just as God appeared in a cloud to confirm the first covenant, Jesus said he would appear in a cloud to remove the first and confirm the second. Why would anyone believe this would be a physical return of Jesus in a physical body?

The passage in Revelation 1 is connected to the one in Acts 1, but not as the futurist doctrine would explain it. John began his Revelation of Jesus Christ by referring to what the angels told the disciples in Acts 1. *"Look, he is coming in the clouds…"* John then added the phrase, *"…and every eye shall see him."* As opposed to the ascension which only a few saw, everyone will "see" his return. John was not saying every person who ever lived would literally see Jesus. He was saying the event of the Lord's return would be such that every person would see that it had happened.

The Greek word "ophthalmos," translated "eye" comes from a "root signifying 'penetration, sharpness' " (Vines Expository

Dictionary of New Testament Words). It can be used to refer to the physical organ, but usually refers to sight in the sense of knowing something, such as in Ephesians 1:18 *"...the eyes of your heart having been enlightened..."*

This is consistent with how the Lord has revealed Himself throughout history. In Exodus 7:4-5, *"Then I will lay my hand on Egypt and with mighty acts of judgment I will bring out my divisions, my people the Israelites. And the Egyptians will know that I am the Lord when I stretch out my hand against Egypt and bring the Israelites out of it."* This passage could be translated "...every eye will see that I am the Lord" and nobody would misunderstand the meaning.

John connected the promise of the angels at the ascension to the prophecy in Zachariah 12:10, *"And I will pour out on the house of David and the inhabitants of Jerusalem a spirit of grace and supplication. They will look on me, the one they have pierced, and they will mourn for him as one mourns for an only child, and grieve bitterly for him as one grieves for a firstborn son."* Zachariah was describing the Lord's coming Judgment on Jerusalem and in 13:1 said, *"On that day a fountain will be opened to the house of David and the inhabitants of Jerusalem, to cleanse them from sin and impurity."* Jerusalem's "cleansing from sin" was fulfilled with Jesus' atonement sacrifice. No other event could do so.

The same concept was used in reference to the establishment of the New Covenant under which "all people" would "know" the Lord. Quoting Jeremiah 31, Hebrews 8:10-12 says, *"This is the covenant I will make with the house of Israel after that time, declares the Lord. I will put my laws in their minds and write them on their hearts. I will be their God, and they will be my people. No longer will a man teach his neighbor, or a man his brother, saying, 'Know the Lord,' because they will all know me, from the least of them to the greatest. For I will forgive their wickedness and will remember their sins no more."*

Obviously not every person in the world knows the Lord, but the New Covenant is for all, not just the Jews, and with the complete revelation of his word, everyone can know him. The concept in both Revelation and in Jesus' predictions of the destruction of Jerusalem and its temple in Matthew 24 is that his coming would be so clear that "every eye will see" it has occurred.

In Matthew 24:27 Jesus said, *"For as lightning that comes from the east is visible even in the west, so will be the coming of the Son of Man."* The destruction of Jerusalem and its temple was an event unlike any other in human history. Just as Daniel and the other Old Testament prophets had predicted, God used the armies of the Roman Empire (Daniel's fourth kingdom or beast) to bring his divine judgment on the nations and ultimately on Jerusalem. The destruction of the temple was known all over the world and has been known by every generation since. Nobody missed this event. It was indeed a "shot heard around the world." Even today one can visit the temple site and will find exactly what Jesus said, *"Not one stone left on top of another."* As lightning from the East can be seen in the West, the absence of the temple is proof of the validity of Scripture and is an everlasting testimony of the completed atonement sacrifice of Jesus. It will never be rebuilt.

So how would anyone know when it happened? Jesus said to watch for the signs.

Matthew 24	Mark 13	Luke 21
₃₂*Now learn this lesson from the fig tree: As soon as its twigs get tender and its leaves come out, you know that summer is near.* ₃₃*Even so, when you see all these things, you know that it is near, right at the door.*	₂₈*Now learn this lesson from the fig tree: As soon as its twigs get tender and its leaves come out, you know that summer is near.* ₂₉*Even so, when you see these things happening, you know that it is near, right at the door.*	₂₉*He told them this parable: "Look at the fig tree and all the trees.* ₃₀*When they sprout leaves, you can see for yourselves and know that summer is near.* ₃₁*Even so, when you see these things happening, you know that the kingdom of God is near.*

When they saw all these things happening around them, they would know. Of course, the final sign of his return, signifying the acceptance by God of his sacrifice confirming that the New Covenant was now in full force and the Holy of Holies was now open to all, was the destruction of the temple. They all saw that!

Jesus said when they saw these signs, they would know that this event was *near*, not two thousand or two million years in the future, *right at the door*. To make sure nobody misunderstood the timing of these events, Jesus concluded his teachings about the signs with the following statement:

Jesus is Coming Soon?

Matthew 24	Mark 13	Luke 21
₃₄*I tell you the truth, this generation will certainly not pass away until all these things have happened.* ₃₅*Heaven and earth will pass away, but my words will never pass away.*	₃₀*I tell you the truth, this generation will certainly not pass away until all these things have happened.* ₃₁*Heaven and earth will pass away, but my words will never pass away.*	₃₂*I tell you the truth, this generation will certainly not pass away until all these things have happened.* ₃₃*Heaven and earth will pass away, but my words will never pass away.*

The generation in which Jesus and his apostles were living was not going to end until *all* these things happened. Many have tried to rationalize this statement of Jesus to mean something entirely different by "stretching" the meaning of "this generation" to some undetermined amount of time that could be centuries long. As pointed out earlier, the Greek word translated here is "genea" from "ginomai" which means "begotten." It refers to the people living during a particular time period. It cannot be changed to indicate a span of thousands of years.

If Jesus had meant a period of unlimited duration, he would have used "aion." He did not. He said exactly what he meant here, which is the same thing he said in Mark 9:1, *"I tell you the truth, some who are standing here will not taste death before they see the kingdom of God come with power."* A look at other passages of Scripture that speak of this generation might be helpful.

Genesis 7:1, *"The Lord then said to Noah, 'Go into the ark, you and your whole family, because I have found you righteous in this generation.'"*

Matthew 11:16-17, *"To what can I compare this generation? They are like children sitting in the marketplaces and calling out to others: 'We played the flute for you, and you did not dance; we sang a dirge and you did not mourn.'"*

Mark 8:12, *"He sighed deeply and said, 'Why does this generation ask for a miraculous sign? I tell you the truth, no sign will be given to it.'"*

Luke 11:30, *"For as Jonah was a sign to the Ninevites, so also will the Son of Man be to this generation."*

Luke 17:25, *"But first he (Jesus) must suffer many things and be rejected by this generation."*

In none of the other passages where "this generation" is used do we have any difficulty with its meaning. Why do we feel the necessity to change its meaning only in the one place where it refers to the coming of the Lord? Jesus said exactly what he meant. That generation would not pass until all these things happened.

Matthew's account of these events is the most lengthy of the three and actually encompasses all of chapters 24 and 25 of his Gospel. To keep the reader on the subject being discussed and not miss the context, he weaved into his text language to connect everything he said to Jesus' discussion of the questions at hand. In 24:10-11 he wrote, *"**At that time** many will turn away from the faith and will betray and hate each other, and many false prophets will appear and deceive many people."* What time? The time when all these buildings would be destroyed. In verse 23, *"**At that time** if anyone says to you, 'Look, here is the Christ!' or, 'There he is!' do not believe it."* What time? Again in verse 30, *"**At that time** the sign of the Son of Man will appear in the sky..."*

In verse 36 he recorded Jesus' words, *"No one knows about **that day or hour**, not even the angels in heaven, nor the Son, but only the*

Father." To what day or hour was he referring? He was still speaking of the time of the destruction of the temple. They would not know the exact day and hour, but they would know it was approaching by watching for the signs.

Some have tried to suggest Jesus' language here does denote a change from his discussion of the destruction of Jerusalem to the end of time, because they would be able to tell when the armies were advancing on Jerusalem, but nobody will know when the final end will come. This interpretation actually denies the very thing Jesus was trying to teach. Neither subject nor context has changed. Jesus' point was they would know by the signs as the end approached, but he was not giving them an exact day and hour.

Much like a woman who announces she is expecting a baby cannot tell you the exact day and hour of the approaching birth. She can tell you it will come within the next nine months. As the time approaches, there will be signs that will narrow the time frame, but they still will not identify the exact hour. When labor begins, she will recognize the signs and know it is time…soon.

This is exactly what Jesus was saying and what we see fulfilled in Scripture. John, who heard his teaching and was watching the signs, wrote in his first letter, *"It is the last hour."* The Revelation given him was about those things that were soon to happen. The time had come. In Revelation 9 we read the four angels *"…who had been kept ready for this very hour and day and month and year were released…"* Finally the exact day and hour had come.

Matthew 25 begins, **"At that time** the kingdom of heaven will be like ten virgins who took their lamps and went out to meet the bridegroom." At what time? Jesus is still speaking of the same time. He concludes this parable with, *"Therefore keep watch, because you do not know* **the day or the hour."**

The parable of the talents begins in verse 14 with these words, **"Again, it will be like** a man going on a journey, who called his servants and entrusted his property to them." What did he mean

again and what was **"it"**? One more example of what that time would be like.

The parable of the sheep and goats starts in verse 30 with, *"When the Son of Man comes in his glory, and all the angels with him, he will sit on his throne in heavenly glory."* This is an obvious reference back to what he had just said in chapter 24 about the coming of the Son of Man. Nowhere in these two chapters does Matthew change the subject. He begins and ends with Jesus' answer to the disciples two questions; "When will these temple buildings be destroyed?" And "...what will be the sign that it is about to happen?" Matthew 26 begins, *"When Jesus had finished all these sayings..."* Not until here does he change the subject.

What Jesus actually said is very clear. Everything he discussed with his apostles was to happen before the end of that generation. God has never made a promise he did not keep. Jesus knew what he was talking about and the apostles understood it and wrote about it in all the subsequent letters that make up the New Testament. Jesus was coming soon...and he did!

CONCLUSION
So What's Next?

One gentleman with whom I discussed these issues asked, "If you are correct and Jesus has already come, then what do we still have to hope for?" It is sad that Christians today have been so inundated with the message of the end of the world and the "soon" coming of Jesus that they believe that is the hope of the gospel message. Nothing could be farther from the truth.

In the first place, Christian teachers and preachers have made so many predictions about the end of the world over the past two centuries that there is little, if any, credibility left in that claim. After all, Jesus did say "I am coming SOON." If he didn't do what he promised to do, why would anyone seriously consider believing any of the Bible?

The "good news" of the gospel of Jesus Christ is forgiveness of sins and eternal life. That is not something for which we hope…it is a present day reality. From the time sin entered the world, generations of people longed for God to fulfill his promise to provide atonement for sin and overcome the power of death. They hoped for the coming Savior.

He came! He made atonement. Hope became reality. We have eternal life. Death has been swallowed up in victory. When Christians leave this physical body they go to heaven to live eternally with God. What greater joy could there possibly be than living in the reality of God's amazing grace, having the full pardon for all our sins, knowing we are in his abiding presence now…and forever!

The hope of the world is, and always has been, its salvation, not its destruction!

Note:

For a more detailed study of the end times, including the resurrection of the dead, the judgement and how the book of Revelation fits into God's eternal plan, one can read *Mystery Accomplished...The Hope of the World* by this same author.

About the Author

Jim Reeves was the youngest of six children. Growing up on a dairy farm in rural Northwest Arkansas shaped his approach to life. His mother was a deeply religious, gentle lady who had an insatiable desire to know and understand the Bible. Her influence made a deep impression on her children and Jim has spent a lifetime following a similar quest.

He graduated from York College with honors and then attended David Lipscomb University in Tennessee where he continued his studies in Bible and music. He also holds a BA in Organizational Management from Concordia University. Jim had a successful career in the oil and gas industry, and has always been actively involved in a local church, having preached, led worship, and taught Bible classes for churches in Arkansas, Indiana, Colorado, and Texas. He and his wife, Donna, were married in 1967 and they have two grown children. They are now retired, living in central Texas.

Jim's professional career took him to several countries and many different cultures around the world, giving him a unique perspective on how the word of God transcends national borders and offers hope and real solutions to people, regardless of their immediate circumstances. He can be contacted via email at jdr.reeves@gmail.com and is always willing to answer questions or study the Scriptures with anyone who is interested.